Summer of My Amazing Luck

Summer of My Amazing Luck

the play

by Chris Craddock

based on the novel
by Miriam Toews

Cover design by Doowah Design.
Photo of Chris Craddock by Ian Jackson of Epic Photography.

This book was printed on Ancient Forest Friendly paper.
Printed and bound in Canada by Marquis Printing.

We acknowledge the support of The Canada Council for the Arts and the Manitoba Arts Council for our publishing program.

National Library of Canada Cataloguing in Publication

Craddock, Chris, 1972-
Summer of my amazing luck / Chris Craddock.

A play.
Adaptation of: Summer of my amazing luck / Miriam Toews.
ISBN 978-1-897109-18-2

I. Toews, Miriam, 1964- . Summer of my amazing luck. II. Title.

PS8555.R238S94 2007 C812'.6 C2007-905044-1

Signature Editions www.signature-editions.com
P.O. Box 206, RPO Corydon, Winnipeg, Manitoba, R3M 3S7

Dedicated to Sheila Squire,
my excellent mom.

Production Notes

Upon reading this script, many directors and producers around Canada have said, "How can we afford this play? It needs five, seven, eleventeen actors or something." This is a fallacy. Our fairly excellent Theatre Network production was done with three, and I feel it was all the better for it. The play could be done with five, seven, eleven people, and if you are involved with a high school or university drama department, I encourage you to do just that. This document, however, will reflect the original production, done with three actors, an unchanging Lucy and two very changing others, a man and a woman, who play Mom, Dad, Lish, the kids, the welfare guy and everyone in between. Our way gave the play a sense of energy and fun, "TYA for adults" as some aptly described it, keeping the audience in mind of the existence of children throughout the production, though they are rarely physically seen.

The stage directions found here will go over just how to do it, in case you would like to do likewise. You may follow them exactly, or treat them as inspiration points, jumping-off places to your own creative production.

The Stage

The stage is covered with toys. On first view, it should seem like the apartment of a harried single parent who cannot keep up with the tidying. In the centre is an old-fashioned kitchen table, reinforced to withstand the activity to come. Two chairs surround it. The table will represent the van, a balcony, a bed, and of course, a table. Beneath it is a plastic box filled with oversized Lego. On stage right is a solid wooden toy box with a hinged lid. Inside are two model vehicles, two small teddy bears, and a monkey puppet. Nearby is a briefcase, a small toy cash register, a Fisher-Price barn, a fedora and a pump-action water gun, as well as Dill's stroller, with a wrapped blanket within to represent Dill. On stage left is a 70's style stepladder seat with a back. Near it sits a laundry basket, holding a small toy guitar, towels and a white piece of fabric for Betty's wedding dress. Behind all this sits a framed scrim, sixteen feet wide and eight feet tall. Behind that sit three stepladders, equipped with black masking. Characters will appear behind it, in memory, dream, fantasy, or to imply physical distance. The sound design is evocative of place and time, supporting with underscoring music when appropriate, as well as sound effects and background noise.

The Performances

Lucy acts as an anchor, grounded and emotionally present, while the two other actors swirl about her, playing multiple characters, often transitioning while onstage. It's okay if the more minor characters are occasionally slightly cartoonish, so long as the more emotionally important characters (Lish, Mom, Dad, Sarah, and Hartley) show up in a more full-blooded form. Half the fun of the production will be in the negotiation of these transitions, not only of character, but of place and time.

The Costumes

Characters tend to be denoted by a simple costume piece that coincides with their base costume. For Lish, it is her black beret. For Dad, a pair of reading glasses, pushed down on the nose. For Lish's Dad, a large pair of gold rimmed spectacles. For Sarah, a grey cardigan, for Mom, a relentless sense of self-reliance. Naomi wears a scarf, while Betty wears a similar scarf as a kerchief for her head. The guards wear aviator sunglasses and Sing wears his accent. You get the idea.

Summer of My Amazing Luck premiered at Theatre Network in Edmonton on April 5, 2005.

Cast
Chris Craddock
Beth Graham
Caroline Livingstone

Director:	Bradley Moss
Dramaturg:	James DeFelice
Set & Costume Designer:	Marissa Kochanski
Lighting Designer:	Scott Peters
Sound Designer:	Dave Clarke
Stage Manager:	Gina Moe

Act One

Lights up on Lucy and Lish in the van. Lish sits on the right side of the table, arms out, steering, a plunger sitting on the table acting as the stick shift. Lucy sits in the passenger seat. She regards the audience.

LUCY:

You probably think you're in a theatre right now, but you're not. You're in a van. You're in a van with two women and five kids. The van is in terrible shape, but it's going from Winnipeg, Manitoba to Denver, Colorado. How we got here is a long story. But isn't that what road trips are for? This story is full of kids, so I might as well start like this...

Once upon a time...

Lucy leaves the van and moves downstage. Lish exits.

...there was a little girl named Lucy. And when you're a little girl, you have all these dreams about how life is going to go, and it's easy to believe it, because nothing has happened to you yet. But it isn't long before stuff starts to happen, and happen, until it seems like life can only go a few ways, and all you can do is hope that one of them is good. You hope that things kind of assemble themselves, and that your life is fun and funny and lucky and good.

Mom and Dad appear behind the scrim. They pose as if for a family portrait.

One of the big things that happened to me is that my mom died, and I didn't grieve right. It made me have a void inside, and then I was promiscuous. If I had grieved right, my doctor said, if I had grieved right, I wouldn't've been sneaking out all the time to fill up my "void," and I wouldn't've been promiscuous. Being promiscuous means I had sex with all these guys, and then I got pregnant. I was really scared, being only seventeen at the time, with a dead mom that I was grieving for all the wrong—

Mom and Dad regard each other as Mom disappears behind the scrim.

LUCY:

—and a dad who wasn't grieving all that good either.

Dad bows his head as the lights go out.

LUCY:

I got pregnant, and then I had a son.

Lucy moves to her stroller and bends down to look at Dill.

LUCY:

A beautiful son named Dill, who I love more than anything. See, Dill was the other big thing that happened to me, and then it was super clear what I had to do. I had to be the best mom an eighteen-year-old with a grade ten education can be. And I know there are women out there who can work a full-time job and raise their kids super well and keep a tidy house besides. I would love to be like that, like one of those formidable women, but I'm not, and I know that. I have a son, who I *love*, and he needs stuff. He needs a home with a crib, and strained peas, and a mobile that spins around and makes him smarter. He needs stuff and so do I. I thought I was totally screwed. But I wasn't.

See, lucky for me, I live in Canada.

A logo of the Canadian flag appears on the scrim. Lucy regards it with a double thumbs-up.

LUCY:

The best country in the world, a generous bear hug of a country, where it's okay to be French, and we even save some of our left-over land for the Indians. Canada's not gonna let a baby starve, just because his grandmother died and his mother didn't grieve right. They got a net for people that fall down, sort of like a circus. A social safety net. And that's where I ended up, feeling just like a trapeze artist that falls.

A trapeze artist balances on the centre upstage stepladder, behind the scrim. She loses her balance and falls, only to be caught by the Welfare Guy.

CANADA:

Whoa! Canada's gotcha!

LUCY:

That's where I am right now. In the social safety net of Canada. In the welfare office.

Welfare Guy enters, flustered and overworked. His shirt is buttoned to the top and he wears large glasses.

WELFARE GUY:
(*shuffling his papers*) Lucy Van Alstyne?

LUCY:
(*enthusiastically*) Yes, hi.

WELFARE GUY:
(*sourly*) Hello.

LUCY:
(*more formally*) Hello, how are you today?

WELFARE GUY:
My name is Leonard. I will be examining your case and ascertaining whether or not you qualify for benefits.

LUCY:
Great.

WELFARE GUY:
Isn't it, though? Oh, goody! Another welfare mom! Oh goody, another mouth to feed. Hey, taxpayers, great news! GOODY!

Pause. Welfare Guy composes himself.

WELFARE GUY:
Let's get started.

LUCY:
And so, we get started. You see, Canada is generous, but responsible. So they ask a lot of questions, and you have to have the right answers. My friend Lish told me one of the first things they ask is:

WELFARE GUY:
The father's name and address?

LUCY:
Pardon?

WELFARE GUY:
Your child's father. His name and address?

Lucy turns to the audience. Welfare Guy freezes.

LUCY:

Now here is a tricky part, because your natural impulse will be to say, of course I know just who the father is.

WELFARE GUY:

You are a good and moral person.

LUCY:

Even though I don't.

Welfare Guy returns to his freeze.

LUCY:

You'll want to say he's a solider who died in the Great War, (*SFX: explosions of war, followed by sentimental music*) but our love was sweet and pure and true.

Welfare Guy listens emotionally and begins weeping.

LUCY:

You'll want to say anything that makes you look like you're not a big slut.

Welfare Guy returns to his freeze.

LUCY:

But if you say you know who the father is, you're dead.

Lish appears behind the scrim, stage right.

LISH:

You're dead! (*overlapping with Lucy's "you're dead"*)

Because then welfare doesn't want to give you the money. They want *you* to get it out of the *father*. And whatever they get him to pay comes right off your cheque. And if he stops paying, it still comes right off your cheque. And sooner or later, they all stop paying. So simplify your life, screw up your courage and say:

I don't know.

LUCY:

I don't know. (*overlapping with Lish's "I don't know."*)

WELFARE GUY:

You don't know.

LUCY:

Um…sorry.

WELFARE GUY:

Well, if you find yourself in a similar situation, I'd advise you to a) utilize some proven form of contraceptive device, or b) obtain the identity of the male, perhaps by asking him his name.

Welfare Guy falls silent, but continues to mouth his lecture to Lucy. Lucy turns to the audience.

LUCY:

Now this is rudeness, and I do feel kinda mad. But when you're on welfare, people are allowed to be rude. I like to pretend I'm a duck's back, and he's water.

WELFARE GUY:

People need to practice self control. I don't go about impregnating people and not leaving my name. I suggest you try to date people more like me.

LUCY:

You're water.

WELFARE GUY:

What?

LUCY:

Yes, sir.

Lish reappears behind the scrim, stage right.

LISH:

Who cares! Just say you don't know who the father is. Hey— If you eat a whole can of beans, how can you know which one made you fart?

Welfare Guy signs the last paper and then stamps it loudly, using a piece of the big Lego as a stamp.

WELFARE GUY:

Take this slip. Take the green line to the right, three lefts, a right and two more lefts, switch to the red line, then two more lefts, a right and a left, switch back to green, two more rights and a left, down the stairs to the elevator, up three floors, then take the stairs down two floors, then the green line splits into *four* lines of *differing shades of green*, yours is *chartreuse*, and it leads to three lefts, a right, and a left to the teller. Where you will receive...your cheque.

LUCY:
Could you say that again?

WELFARE GUY:
(*laughing*) No.

LUCY:
Please?

WELFARE GUY:
No nonny no no.

LUCY:
Come on, Leonard…

WELFARE GUY:
Do you know what time it is?

LUCY:
No.

WELFARE GUY:
It's No time. NEXT!

Lucy does laps with her stroller, struggling with her directions. Welfare Guy turns upstage, unbuttons his shirt and removes his glasses. The teller, in a wig and sweater vest, comes onto stage. She takes two inflated balls out of the basket and puts them in her sweater to represent her breasts. She moves the stage right stepladder to form the barrier of her teller's kiosk. She will speak in a Scottish accent. Welfare Guy becomes Lucy's fellow welfare recipient and is in front of Lucy in line. A short silent pantomime of disappointment is acted out between the teller and this welfare recipient under Lucy's speech below.

LUCY:
The tellers are behind two-inch bulletproof glass and you don't have to talk to them, which is good because it gives me a chance to look tough like the other ladies here.

The first welfare recipient leaves and then rejoins the line as a new character.

LUCY:
Dill starts to freak out, so I start to breast-feed him. Then I see a sign that says—

TELLER:

No breast-feeding allowed on the premises.

LUCY:

So I pull my boob out of Dill's mouth, and it makes a little (*SFX:thok!*) sound and a little jet of breast milk squirts out before I can get my boob back into my feeding bra.

Lucy's fellow welfare recipient takes a small water pistol out of his pocket. He aims from Lucy's chest and shoots three times into the audience, representing breast milk.

LUCY:

I hear somebody say—

SOMEBODY:

That's disgusting.

LUCY:

So I breathe. That's other thing you can do, if the duck's back thing isn't working, is breathing—

TELLER:

AHEM.

LUCY:

And I've got that teller I've been hearing about.

TELLER:

Now, I'm not one to judge others, but people who get this welfare are like pus-y scabs on the ass of Christ. Not that I judge. Jesus said, judge not, lest you get judged, and he'll judge you, oh, he's judging you *right now*.

The Teller continues to mouth words as Lucy speaks.

LUCY:

I am so close to getting my cheque I can just taste it. Here she comes. She's gonna give it to me. If she can just give me my cheque, I will kiss her for gratitude.

TELLER:

Here's your dirty money.

A sudden and loud "Hallelujah" chorus plays as Lucy lifts her cheque to the heavens.

LUCY:

And everything is okay! My baby can eat and she wasn't rude again, and—

SFX: Hallelujah chorus cuts out suddenly.

TELLER:

Not that you deserve it.

LUCY:

That is so rude. Why— Why would you say that? That is just—

TELLER:

Security! SECURITY!

The Teller and others scatter from Lucy as she escapes, doing a lap in her stroller.

LUCY:

Breathing and a duck's back, and walking quickly out the door. But I am not done yet. I have another mission to accomplish today.

The Mission Impossible theme plays. Light comes up on the Agent, behind the scrim, centre.

AGENT:

Your mission, should you choose to accept it, is to pay your phone bill before the line gets cut off and you lose your only affordable pleasure, that of making local calls. You have twenty minutes to get to the phone place in the mall before it closes. Your stroller will self-destruct in five seconds.

Lights down on the Agent.

LUCY:

The stroller wheel that always falls off seems to be staying on today, so I decide to risk a trip to the mall. Halfway there, the wheel falls off. But I don't have time to fix it, so I grab it up and Dill does a wheelie to the mall.

One actor moves to the stage right stepladder seat. He moves it perpendicular to the stage and then kneels on it, facing Lucy. He assumes the manner of a robot, and holds children's bongo drums at his chest. Lucy taps the drum with her fingertip to represent the buttons, and then puts the cheque into his open mouth.

LUCY:

I put my cheque in the bank machine and try to get cash back out for the phone bill.

LUCY:

But I can't because—

BANK MACHINE:

You don't have a previous balance. Loser.

LUCY:

So it won't give me any money for five days until the cheque clears. The bank machine tells me to:

BANK MACHINE:

Have a nice day!

LUCY:

And then Dill pitches his body back that way he does, and the broken stroller falls backwards.

The Bank Machine reaches out and violently pushes over the stroller. An old lady enters from stage left.

LUCY:

(*visibly upset*) Dill starts screaming and I am breathing while I help him, I'm a duck's back, and I hear this old lady say:

OLD LADY:

That is terrible parenting.

LUCY:

(*calm*) And that's IT.

Lucy stands centre and screams to the heavens, heavily supported by the SFX. Metal guitar starts to play. The Bank Machine becomes a bystander, shocked at Lucy's outburst, as is the old lady.

LUCY:

I pull Dill out of the stroller and start kicking it.

Lucy mime-kicks the stroller. The bystander picks it up and slams it down, as if Lucy's kick has done it.

LUCY:

People are looking at me like I'm crazy, but I don't care. I kick it all the way to the fountain in the middle of the mall and then I pick it up and throw it in.

Lucy picks up one end of the stroller. The bystander picks up the other end. Lucy spins with it and lets go. The bystander slow motions the arc of the throw, timing the descent to match a large SPLASH *from the sound design.*

LUCY:

Then I march right into the Bay and right to the first floor model stroller I see. It's beautiful. It costs more than I get for the month and it pushes like a dream. And I know, because I push it right out of the Bay and right outside and I don't stop until I get home. Dill gurgles the whole way. He likes his new stroller. He's happy.

I hope he doesn't remember this. I don't want him to be a thief. Just an outlaw.

Music. Actors emerge and create the Have-a-Life environment. Lucy does a lap in her stroller and arrives at Have-a-Life.

LUCY:

This is where I live. It's not much to look at, but it's home and I can afford it. How you ask? With the help of Canada. See, this is public housing, in the centre of Winnipeg, in the centre of Canada, the centre of the world. Geographically. Ours is called "Have-a-Life" which sucks ass as a name, if you ask me. We call it:

NAOMI:

Half-a-Life.

LUCY:

And.

TERRAPIN:

Have-a-Laugh.

LUCY:

And other stuff like that. It's mostly poor single women, trying hard to raise their kids.

NAOMI:

Hey, Lucy!

LUCY:

Hey, Naomi! How's Tina?

NAOMI:

Good. Nice stroller.

LUCY:

Thanks. Naomi's husband was a nice guy, but a drunk. He died choking on his own vomit. Now she lives here. She's not on welfare. She's one of the working poor. Which is way harder, but you get slightly more respect. She lives across from Terrapin.

TERRAPIN:

Lucy!

LUCY:

That's her. She's a hippie. Her husband ran off with a Jefferson Airplane tribute band.

TERRAPIN:

Lucy, I'm having a solstice party. You must come.

LUCY:

Great. When is it?

TERRAPIN:

It's a *solstice* party.

LUCY:

Cool. When's it gonna be?

TERRAPIN:

(*sighs and looks at her*)

LUCY:

What?

NAOMI:

Hairpin, are you being an asshole to Lucy?

TERRAPIN:

(*crosses to Naomi*) She doesn't know when solstice is.

NAOMI:

Terrapin, every day I spend with you is the longest day of the year.

Terrapin walks off in a huff and does a lap; soon she will be Sarah. Naomi sits and transforms into Sing, grabbing a toy guitar.

LUCY:

They don't get along. Like, at all.

SING:

(*singing*) Look out, kid. They know what you did, don't know when, but you're doing it again!

LUCY:

Hey, Sing!

SING:

Hello, Lucy!

LUCY:

He's the caretaker. His real name is Bhupinder Singh Dhillon, but we just call him Sing, I guess 'cause it's easier, and 'cause he sings. Mostly Dylan.

SING:

(singing) They want eleven dollar bills but you've only got ten.

Sarah comes out, writing a Post-It note. She hands it to Sing. Sing reads it and nods.

LUCY:

Hey, Sarah!

Sarah waves.

Sarah doesn't talk.

Sing and Sarah exit together.

LUCY:

There's a reason for that, but I'll tell you later.

Lucy walks on and comes upon Lish, doing a yoga sequence. Lish doesn't seem to see her.

LUCY:

And Lish. The most interesting person I ever knew. My best friend since I got here. She's amazing. She could have been a star on the stage but "her lust interfered with her passion." That's what she said. Now she makes scenes out of her life, and I have a front row seat.

LISH:

(*notices her*) Hey, Luce. Did you steal that stroller?

LUCY:

Yeah.

LISH:

You magnificent bitch! Hey, Dill, let's go show the girls.

Lish checks out the stroller and rolls it off stage. Lucy turns to the audience.

LUCY:

And this is where I live, thanks to my mom dying and me not grieving right.

...My mom.

Mom appears at the upstage table, napping, with a spoon in her hand.

If my mom got tired she would take a nap sitting up at the kitchen table with a spoon in her hand. And when the spoon fell, the noise would wake her up and she would be totally refreshed.

Mom drops the spoon and awakens with a start. She gets up, immediately alert, standing and walking quickly to her briefcase, picking it up, turning, and exiting.

LUCY:

Power napping, she called it. Life was funny to her.

Mom appears centre, behind the screen.

MOM:

Good luck!

LUCY:

She always used to say that. It was an all-purpose wish she'd send us off with. (*waving*) Mom, I'm going to school.

MOM:

Good luck!

LUCY:

Mom, I'm taking out the garbage.

MOM:

Good luck!

LUCY:

Mom, I want a car for my birthday.

MOM:

(*laughing*) Good luck!

LUCY:

She said it just like she was saying—

MOM:

Fuck you!

LUCY:

But she was always saying—

MOM:

Good luck!

LUCY:

I wonder if it came true. I wonder if she would think my life was lucky. I wonder if she would be disappointed in me.

Mom comes onto stage. This was the last time Lucy saw her mother.

MOM:

Lucy, have you seen my car keys? I have to get going.

LUCY:

(*a little reluctant*) On the table, Mom.

MOM:

Well, look at that. I'm off, Lucy. I love you.

LUCY:

I wish—

MOM:

Up north for a week. Back on Monday.

LUCY:

I wish you didn't have to go.

MOM:

I know. But it seems that I do. So— Good! Luck!

Mom exits.

LUCY:

Mom died on her way out of town to go counsel farm women whose husbands beat them. That was her job. She was a family therapist. The main thing she did for the women was tell them—

Mom and a patient appear behind the scrim on two of the stepladders.

MOM:

(*with a patient*) Leave your husband! Just go! Take your kids and get away. Just leave him. Leave your husband!

PATIENT:

(*crying*) Okay.

LUCY:

But it's not good to just come right out and say that. So mostly she just said—

MOM:

Uh huh?

PATIENT:

Bwah!

LUCY:

Or:

MOM:

Continue.

PATIENT:

Bwah ha!

LUCY:

Or:

MOM:

And how did that make you feel?

PATIENT:

BWAAAAAAAAAAAAHHH!

LUCY:

And it took nine or ten months of saying stuff like that to get them to leave their husbands on their own. She saw patients in my old playroom. I was always hearing the strangest shouting and crying.

PATIENT:

(*crying gibberish*) And when I see that dah bah dye— And some dum ba fo do po— I just wanna grab an, an, an break with the fo and the jonny, I say to him, and he does, and what I no, and I just RUM! DAN! BUR! FUM! And he just foom, you no? On fire?

MOM:

Yeah.

LUCY:

I think Dad always kind of resented all the unstable people that would come through the house.

Dad comes onto the stage, crossing angrily to the table.

LUCY:

When they were there, he would start to mow the lawn.

He starts the chair like a lawn mower, picking it up and mowing the lawn with it.

LUCY:

He would mow a lot right outside the window where Mom saw patients. It was like he was trying to say—

Dropping the lawn mower and turning into a quickly appearing spotlight.

DAD:

Go away from here! Take your pain and disappointment and leave us be! Can't you see we have enough of our own? Why must you be so weak? Just do as I do. Take your rage and…mow the lawn.

Dad mows the lawn back and forth, energetically.

LUCY:

Our lawn looked so trim that summer. In fact it was kind of bald and patchy. Sometimes he wouldn't mow the lawn. He would do the dishes.

Dad parks the "lawnmower," and picks up a box of Lego. He picks up "dishes" and slams them on the table.

LUCY:

My friends would say, that's nice your dad does dishes. But he wasn't doing them to be nice. He was doing them to be loud.

Mom enters. She glares at Dad and snatches the dish from his hand. She starts spitting in the "dishes," throwing each one offstage.

LUCY:

One time my mom spit in every dish he had washed and threw them into the backyard, while Dad stood there and said—

DAD:

What are you doing? What are you doing?

Mom exits. Dad cleans up the dishes sadly.

LUCY:

Mom wore the pants in the family. Not that my dad wore skirts, he just wasn't the boss. Of anything, anywhere, it seemed. He taught geology, so I guess he could run a classroom, but he was no match for Mom.

Dad sits with some Lego, put together to represent a piece of paper.

LUCY:

Our house was built on a double lot, and the extra room had the most beautiful chokecherry trees, and Saskatoon berries, and flowers Dad had planted, and his love for them was a lot more obvious than his love for us. But this neighbouring car dealership wanted to buy the land.

Mom enters and sits at the table with Dad. She silently requests the letter and reads it.

LUCY:

They wrote a letter and said that the city would rezone it as commercial and we would have to sell it anyway for way less than they were offering. Mom said—

MOM:

Be a man! Get a lawyer, write a letter. It's important to you, so stand up for it! Do something.

DAD:

I don't want to fight.

MOM:

Fine. Let them bulldoze your precious trees and flowers. See if I care.

Dad breaks down in tears.

LUCY:

And then Dad put his head down by his Cheerios and started to cry. It was awful.

MOM:

Oh, for Pete's sake.

Mom stands and moves away from the table.

LUCY:

I had never seen a grown-up cry before, let alone my dad.

DAD:

I'm sorry. I'm sorry.

Dad exits.

LUCY:

He stayed in bed for a week when the backhoes came. He had Mom cancel his classes, and he just hid. That's what he was always doing when he was home.

Hiding.

Mom drove all over the province to counsel in this community or that, and she had this terrible habit of picking up hitchhikers. We all told her it was crazy. I mean, didn't she read the papers? She would only pick up ones that had bags. She said the ones with bags are serious. And one day she picked up one of her serious hitchhikers with a bag, but instead of a bag of sweatshirts and AC/DC tapes, it was a bag of knives and guns. Mom did everything so fast, I bet she died fast too. I hope so. She hated waiting. Mom could make a tuna sandwich in three minutes and a pot of coffee in one. She'd say—

Mom appears behind the scrim, at centre.

MOM:

Well. If that was lunch, I've had it.

Funeral music comes up. Dad shuffles up to Lucy and they sit beside each other, Dad leaning heavily on Lucy.

LUCY:

I thought that would be a good thing to put on her tombstone. But I couldn't see us all crying in front a grave like that. Things like that don't happen. The minister kept telling us to celebrate the life.

Dad starts to cry, hard and openly.

LUCY:

But Dad just leaned on me in the front row and cried and cried. I thought, what is he gonna do without her? What am I gonna do without him?

DAD:

I'm sorry. I'm sorry.

Dad exits, leaving Lucy alone.

LUCY:

I figure somewhere in here I started to develop my void.

Lish enters with a triangle and a flyswatter. She clears her throat. Lucy looks up.

LUCY:

Oh. Lish's Story.

Lish does a beginning move of her interpretive dance, which Lucy punctuates with a strike of the triangle. Music comes up and Lish does a modern dance, interpreting the story Lucy is telling about her.

LUCY:

Once upon a time, there was a magical creature, a woman so lovely and strange that men could not help but get her pregnant. Her parents were rich, but conservative, and seeing her condition, they kicked her out of the house, refusing to give her any money. Her father said:

Lish's Dad appears behind the scrim at centre.

LISH'S DAD:

You got yourself into this. You can get yourself out.

LUCY:

Alone, with no support, she soon found herself with only Canada to rely upon, and she moved here, to Have-a-Life. She was a fantastic and funny mother, and in her spare time, she enjoyed helping others. She volunteered for many arts groups and charities, and she was doing so at the Winnipeg Street Performers Festival when she fell irretrievably in love with a juggler named Gotcha.

Gotcha dances in, juggling scarves. Lucy strikes the triangle and they see each other for the first time. They begin to dance together, sexy and fun.

LUCY:

She already had two children, Maya and Hope, when she met this wandering rogue, and so even though Gotcha begged Lish to run away with him, a life as a performer was even less practical for her than it ever is. And so Lish and the juggler were limited to one fateful week together in the festival hotel. In wistful times, Lish was heard to remark:

Their dance freezes, in a compromising position.

LISH:

I'd do anything to see this guy again. To wrap my hairy legs around his hot back and to see him juggle for his daughters.

LUCY:

And other times—

LISH:

It's better not to know. Once you know, you care, and once you care, you've lost.

She spins away from Gotcha, and crumples to the ground, sleeping. Gotcha looks back and forth, and then steals her wallet. He leaves at a run.

LUCY:

And well she might speak that way, for when Lish awoke in that hotel room, she found that Gotcha was gone. He had stolen her wallet, and left her with only a note.

Behind the scrim, left.

GOTCHA:

Catch you on the flip side.

Lights down on Gotcha.

LUCY:

But little did he know, he had also left a gift. The gift of special sperm. The magic kind that makes not one baby, but two.

Lish pulls scarves out of her pockets to represent Gotcha's sperm.

LUCY:

Sperm destined to become Letitia and Alba. But Lish did not know this at the time. She shrugged off the loss of her wallet and stole a room service spoon for revenge.

Lucy slides a spoon across the floor towards Lish. Lish grabs it.

LISH:

AHA!

LUCY:

Later, when the twins were born, they would be heard to remark:

Letitia enters to find Alba playing with the spoon, balancing it on her nose.

LETITIA:

It's my turn to play with Daddy's spoon!

Letitia takes the spoon and runs off to play, leaving Lish on the floor.

LUCY:

And it was all the memento they needed of the father they never knew. But secretly, Lish harboured a dark and brooding love for the juggler, a love that knew no limits, a love that tortured her still for the lack of it, and perhaps would do so…forever.

A little harpsichord takes us out of storytelling. Lish is left on the floor, crying.

LUCY:

But I hoped it wouldn't. Lish was my best friend. And she was crying an awful lot in those days, all locked in her room. Her kids were walking around like in a funeral home, with gentle eyes that are worried underneath.

Alba enters.

ALBA:

Shhh, Lucy. Mommy's having a good cry. (*worried look*) Again.

LUCY:

On the table I found a copy of the Winnipeg Street Performers Festival program, 1992, and Gotcha's picture was circled about a hundred thousand times. Seeing Lish fall all apart filled me with a crazy kind of panic. I couldn't help but think that if Lish couldn't be happy, I was never gonna be. Her fate and mine seemed all tied together, and so, even though I knew it wasn't right, I made a plan. And I called my plan: "The Return of Gotcha," and unfortunately, it involved lying. Back when I was a kid, I had tried something like this before.

Lish exits. Lucy moves to centre.

LUCY:

The way it worked last time was, my cousin Delia (*Delia joins Lucy*) and I played a trick on my other cousin, David.

David enters on a skateboard.

LUCY:

There was this girl he liked, and he wouldn't shut up about her.

David talks excitedly to his mom.

DAVID:

And I gave her a double all the way to the Mac's and we talked about school and stuff and she has hair like Farrah Fawcett and I really like her and I think she likes me, I think she likes me, I hope she does because she held my hand in Science class, and she already went through puberty!

LUCY:

And so me and Delia decided to write a fake letter from the girl that David liked. We wrote it all in big swoopy letters like a girl her age would and it went like this:

Delia takes a step forward to become Sandy. David reads along.

SANDY:

Dear David. I like you a lot. Happy face. Please meet me at the Mohawk after school if you like me too. And if you don't already have a girlfriend. Sad Face. Love, Sandy.

David finishes reading and jumps up and down with excitement. He runs off.

LUCY:

And then we dropped the letter in the mailbox and waited. We were so excited. After school we waited for David to come through the door. And then he did.

David slowly rolls on, crushed

All he said was:

DAVID:

(*soft*) Hey.

LUCY:

And that was it. We had broken his little heart. We felt so bad, we told him what we did and we apologized. All he said was:

DAVID:

'Kay.

LUCY:

And so we apologized harder and Delia even said:

DELIA:

We were assholes.

Lucy and Delia gasp.

LUCY:

And neither of us had ever said that word out loud before, so we hoped it would convince him that we were extra super sorry, but he just said:

DAVID:

'Kay.

David moves to one side, turning his skateboard into a paddle. Delia turns her hat, becoming a disturbed teen.

LUCY:

Today he's married and almost bald and he helps disturbed teens by canoeing with them.

DAVID:

Hey, canoeing!

The teen makes a demon face and gives him the finger. David looks out helplessly. They exit.

LUCY:

But the point is that it was a solid idea, just used in the wrong spirit. This time I will use my powers for good, rather than evil. And Lish needed this. She needed a nice fake letter.

SFX: Thunderclap and rain. Lucy opens an umbrella.

LUCY:

And we all needed something. Like umbrellas, maybe. It was raining all the time those days, like God was taking a tremendous beer piss on our heads. The mosquito population had used the extra moisture to double and triple and quadruple itself and once you started slapping, you lost and had to go inside. And at night, if you were real quiet, you could hear people scratching their bites. Tons of basements around here were flooding and Sing was digging a trench to take the water away, but nobody knew to where.

Sing appears behind the scrim, shoveling, being sheltered by an umbrella held by Sarah.

SING:

(*singing*) Red rain is coming down! Red rain!

LUCY:

The Red River and Assiniboine were fat up against the banks, and the news said there was more rain to come yet.

Lish enters.

LUCY:

So when Lish said:

Lish enters in the rain. She puts her hand out, and lights and sound shift sharply to a beautiful day.

LISH:

Lucy, come out! The sun is shining!

LUCY:

It was like a French kiss from Jesus.

LISH:

God, that feels good.

LUCY:

Yeah.

LISH:

Walk me to the mailbox?

LUCY:

(*gives an excited look to the audience*) Sure.

LISH:

I'm walking on sunshine, oh oh!

LUCY:

Lish was sort of a terrible singer.

LISH:

I'm walking on sunshine, oh oh!

LUCY:

And we got to the mailbox.

The actor comes out and lifts the Fisher-Price house to his face. The postcard is within.

LISH:

And don't it feel good! Oh!

LUCY:

Key is in.

LISH:

All right now! And don't it feel good!

LUCY:

Mail is out.

LISH:

You bet now! And don't it feel— oh, my God.

"Mailbox" puts down the house and exits.

LUCY:

(*a little too naïve*) What is it, Lish?

LISH:

Oh, my God, this is too weird.

LUCY:

Oh, my gosh, Lish, what is it?

LISH:

It's from Gotcha. It's from him.

LUCY:

Oh, my God, Lish—

LISH:

I know!

LUCY:

What does it say?

LISH:

Uh, it says:

Gotcha appears behind the scrim, centre. He is wearing a porkpie hat and juggling three balls.

GOTCHA:

Hey, Baby. Long time no see. Sorry I took your wallet back then. I was going through a really rough time. But if I didn't have your wallet I wouldn't have your address, would I? I guess I never quite forgot about you. Nobody ever made me laugh like you did. I'm traveling around a lot so don't try to write me. I'm in Cleveland right now, but not for long. Bye for now. Love, GOTCHA!

LISH:

That crazy freak. He must assume that I know his name.

LUCY:

Yeah.

LISH:

He is one terrible writer.

LUCY:

Oh. Do you think?

LISH:

Oh, yeah.

LUCY:

(*disappointed*) Huh.

LISH:

That crazy freak.

LUCY:

So Lish. How do you feel?

LISH:

(*happy girlish squeal*) AHHHHHHHHHHHHHHHHHHHH!

Lish does a little dance in the rain and exits.

LUCY:

It worked. My plan completely worked.

SFX: Thunder and rain

LUCY:

And then it started to rain again.

Lish quick-changes into Sarah offstage, changing her signature beret for a grey sweater. Sarah enters with an umbrella.

LUCY:

They say in every life a little rain must fall. And for some of us, that's extra true.

Sarah doesn't talk. She can, but she doesn't. She smiles and laughs, and when she needs to relay information, she does it with little Post-It notes. Once she gave me one that said:

SFX: (Sarah's recorded voice) If you knew what I was thinking about right now, you'd laugh for a week.

LUCY:

And I keep it on my fridge. Sarah has a son named Emmanuel, and he's the most beautiful little boy you ever saw, no matter where he came from. You see—

Sarah stops Lucy with a hand on her arm. Lucy nods and gestures for Sarah to continue. Sarah steps forward.

SARAH:

You see, I was from one of those houses. One of those houses that nobody wants to talk about, where terrible things happen and everybody knows and pretends they don't. These things went on for years, and I knew no one would believe me, but when I got pregnant, I thought, here it is. Here's the proof. Now they would help me. And I told everybody who the father was, but nobody wanted to hear it. Everybody said I must be crazy to say such things about the man that raised me, that I was a crazy, ungrateful girl and I told hurtful lies, and a tramp besides, and that I should go away, get out, get out of our house. So I decided, standing on that porch, that if no one believes me about the most important thing, I wouldn't waste words about food or weather. I wouldn't say another word, ever again. And that's what I did. I moved here to Have-a-Life, and me and Emmanuel were just fine. We were fine. Until—

Sarah is overcome. Lucy consoles her for a second and continues the story.

LUCY:

Until a social worker found out the whole sad story.

The social worker enters, crossing to Sarah.

LUCY:

He decided that Emmanuel was in terrible psychological danger. The social worker said:

SOCIAL WORKER:

Emmanuel must know the truth, or he'll grow up replete with an unfocused rage, and will most likely spend his life in prison. Yes, he must be told the truth, and you, you need to start talking.

Sarah writes a note on a Post-It and hands it to the social worker.

SOCIAL WORKER:

(*crumpling note*) There is no need for profanity.

The social worker spins and drops to his knees, becoming Emmanuel, listening to his mother.

LUCY:

So Emmanuel was told, which freaked him right out and Sarah started talking, which freaked him out even more. He didn't want to go to school and Sarah didn't want to make him, so after he missed a few days, Social Services came back.

Emmanuel stands and becomes the social worker.

LUCY:

Sarah lost her temper and yelled at them and that is absolutely not allowed.

The social worker takes Emmanuel by his shoulders and exits with him. Sarah follows, distraught, stopping just short of exiting.

LUCY:

So now Emmanuel is in a foster home, and Sarah only gets a ninety-minute supervised visit every other weekend. Isn't that the saddest thing you ever heard? Sarah prepares for those visits like she's meeting the love of her life—

Sarah turns, waiting for Emmanuel. She sees him and waves.

LUCY:

—because…she is.

Sarah exits, quick-changing into Lish.

LUCY:

Things happen, and most of the time it is no one's fault. But sometimes it is.

LISH:

(*entering*) It's all Sindy's fault.

They direct the rest at the Fisher-Price house, which now represents Serenity Place.

LUCY:

Sindy McCormican lives one project over, at Serenity Place.

LISH:

She told that social worker.

LUCY:

You don't tell on people who aren't hurting people.

LISH:

It's against the code. She broke the code.

LUCY:

Poor Sarah.

LISH:

I know.

LUCY:

I can't believe it.

LISH:

Don't worry. She'll get hers. You wait and see.

LUCY:

I hope so.

LISH:

They all will. They're evil.

LUCY:

Those ladies at Serenity Place…

LISH:

They're not like us.

LUCY:

I hate them.

LISH:

Sure. We all do.

LUCY:

Serenity Place sucks.

LISH:

Sucks ass.

LUCY:

Yeah!

LISH:

Don't worry. They'll get theirs. You wait and see.

Lish exits.

LUCY:

And now, it's a feud. All of us at Have-a-Life hate all them at Serenity Place, and they hate us, forever and ever. It doesn't even make any sense. It's like Israel and Palestine. Except we're *both* poor.

Lish pops out from behind the scrim.

LISH:

Lucy, put on your best T-shirt. We're going out to dinner.

A waiter comes out with a blanket. He puts it over the table like a tablecloth.

LUCY:

The return of Gotcha had gone great. Lish wasn't crying at all now. In fact, she wanted to celebrate. She decided to take us all out, using the forty-eight dollars in quarters she had for laundry.

Lish enters with the Lego box, representing the bag of quarters.

LUCY:

We drank red wine and she recounted the blissful week her and Gotcha had spent together almost five years ago.

Both of the girls sit, the waiter holding chairs out from them. He claps his hands and restaurant lighting and sound appears. He disappears behind the table.

LISH:

He was one of those very solemn lovemakers. Very serious.

LUCY:

Serious?

LISH:

Yeah. I had to pretend all my laughing was moaning. I wonder if he knew.

The waiter becomes Dill, popping his head out from the downstage side of the table.

LUCY:

Dill was crawling around to other tables and the girls were performing a play about two British women getting drunk. The dialogue was pretty repetitive.

Lish drops to her knees, becoming Alba. Dill pops up behind the table as Letitia.

ALBA:
Oh, I'm drunk.

LETITIA:
Ooooh, I am also drunk.

ALBA:
Let's drink more beer.

LETITIA:
Yummy yummy beer.

They giggle and disappear.

LUCY:
You've seen people like us in restaurants, and you always wish that we would control our damn kids. Well, that night, in that restaurant, that was us. That was us all over. And then the manager came over.

Alba stands behind the table as the Manager. He is buttoned right up and speaks in a heavy French accent.

MANAGER:
Madam, I apologize, but I am concerned for the other patrons and the disturbance your children seem to be causing them.

LISH:
You're concerned?

MANAGER:
I am.

LISH:
And you have come to intercede on behalf of these patrons?

MANAGER:
I'm afraid so.

LISH:
These adults have asked you to come over here to officially protest the existence of my children.

MANAGER:
Well, not their existence—

LISH:

Their presence then. Their presence in this restaurant.

MANAGER:

(*relieved*) Yes, exactly.

LISH:

I see.

LUCY:

Poor sap. He had no idea.

LISH:

This is a public place, is it not?

MANAGER:

Yes, of course.

LISH:

And my children are people, for the most part, are they not?

MANAGER:

Well—

LISH:

And being people, they are part of the public, are they not? Am I misusing the word? The public means all people, regardless of race, gender, religion or age? Or am I wrong?

MANAGER:

All I am saying—

LISH:

All you're saying is that your restaurant discriminates against the young. Is that not exactly what you're saying?

MANAGER:

Not on purpose…

LISH:

No, you would never say such a thing on purpose. It would be offensive and illegal, but that is in fact what is happening here, isn't it? My children are being discriminated against, for nothing more than the relative recentness of their birth!

MANAGER:

No, I—

LISH:

(*standing*) WHY DON'T YOU BURN A CROSS ON MY LAWN?

LUCY:

Here we go...

LISH:

You know, you people remind me of the other people. You know the people I mean, Lucy?

LUCY:

(*like an unwilling actor in a familiar scene*) What people do you mean, Lish?

LISH:

The people who put up signs in their stores that say *No Strollers*, when what they really mean is— no women with children. And especially no poor women who have to haul their lives about in their disturbingly second-hand strollers, uncomfortably reminding passersby that life is sometimes difficult for the less fortunate!

LUCY:

(*weakly*) Testify!

LISH:

I'd like to see a sign that says *No Suits. No Toupees. No Body Odour.* Let me tell you, sir, if there were any of those signs on this restaurant, you would not be standing here now.

MANAGER:

I'll have to ask you to leave.

LISH:

You'd have to beg us to stay!

MANAGER:

Here is your bill.

LISH:

Oh, I see. You'd like us to pay you for ruining our evening. Well, then. I'd be only too happy.

LUCY:

And then Lish took her huge bag of quarters, and:

Lish lifts the box of Lego and empties it on the table. SFX: Coins falling.

LISH:

Keep the change. Come on, Lucy! We're leaving!

Lish marches out of the restaurant. The manager grabs all four corners of the tablecloth and clears it and the Lego. He exits.

LUCY:

Like I say, Lish could have been an actress. And you might wonder why I did whatever she said, and let her drag me on these sometimes kind of embarrassing adventures, but I think it's 'cause—she reminded me a bit of my mom. She's got that same thing my mom did. Too much energy. Not enough life…

Two Brazilian soap opera stars appear behind the scrim, right. They are in a lover's quarrel, spoken in gibberish Portugese.

LUCY:

In Brazil, they let the audience vote on what is going to happen in the soap operas. You get to call in and help decide if Rosita is going to stick with her husband, Dr. Perez, or if she is gonna run off with the handsome Captain Hombre.

She slaps him several times. He carries her off.

LUCY:

But if I were Brazilian, I would vote for everybody to get together and stay. I would vote for living happily ever after, for all of us.

Sarah had a meeting with Social Services this very day, to talk about getting Emmanuel back. She was really nervous and me and Lish were coaching her. Okay, mostly Lish.

Lish enters. Sarah is unseen.

LISH:

Tell them you're looking for a job compatible with parenting, because you don't consider welfare to be a career option.

LUCY:

That's good. And tell them that you are hoping someday to work in the helping profession—

LISH:

Right—because in your experience they are all doing such a good job. And tell them that you understand the mistakes that were made and your part in it, and that even though it won't be easy you're going to do your best to—uh—

LUCY:

To provide a positive home environment for Emmanuel.

LISH:

You're learning the lingo, Lucy.

LUCY:

Thank you very much.

LISH:

You go get 'em, Sarah!

LUCY:

Good luck!

LISH:

You always say that.

LUCY:

I always wish that.

LISH:

Fair enough.

LUCY:

I do. And if I were Brazilian I would vote for good luck for all of us. We all would.

Naomi enters with a newspaper.

NAOMI:

Holy fucking shit, you guys, look at this!

LUCY:

But I guess we'd lose, 'cause Naomi burst in with a newspaper just then. And everybody crowded around and read the article and said stuff like :

LISH:

That filthy, filthy BLEEP!

A sound effect censors the word, in this case, the C-word. The effects are made verbally, by the actor who isn't swearing at the moment. Lucy is exempt from this exercise.

LUCY:

(*reacting to the swearing*) Oh!— And stuff that's worse than that. I didn't think there *was* stuff worse than that, but there is.

LISH:

How can she do this to us?

NAOMI:

She can do it because it's politically popular to do it!

LUCY:

What's going on?

LISH:

What's going on is the Minister of Welfare—

NAOMI:

Bunnie Hutchinson.

LISH:

Bunnie BLEEP Hutchinson—

NAOMI:

Bunnie BLEEP-ing Hutchinson is gonna take away our child tax credit, on account of we don't BLEEP-ing deserve it—

LISH:

On account of we're on the BLEEP-ing welfare.

LUCY:

The child tax credit— I'll explain, because they just swear the whole time—

NAOMI AND LISH:

Mother-BLEEP-er!

LUCY:

—the child tax credit is worth about fifteen hundred bucks, which is a major big deal when your annual income is nine thousand six hundred like mine is. And normal moms still get the tax credit. It's just us welfare moms that don't.

LISH:

Bunnie BLEEP-ing Hutchinson—

LUCY:

And it was all her idea. In a flash, the news was all over the block. Everybody was super depressed, but nobody knew what to do. Terrapin said:

Lish passes her beret to Lucy and becomes Terrapin.

TERRAPIN:

I am going to go down to the legislature right now and chain myself to the buffalo statue out front.

NAOMI:

It's a bison, Nellie McClung.

TERRAPIN:

Oh, that is it!

Naomi and Terrapin start a slapping fight. Terrapin leaves to become Lish, leaving Naomi maintaining the illusion with slaps.

LUCY:

Guys, stop it! Fighting won't help. And Lish said:

LISH:

Yeah, she's right. Fighting won't help. Nothing's going to change. We might as well just get fucking drunk.

Naomi BLEEPS too late. Lish looks at her as if to say, What the hell? Naomi shrugs and moves upstage. She moves her scarf up into a kerchief and becomes Betty.

LUCY:

And she was right. What else was there to do? We didn't have any power. I was barely old enough to vote. How come none of the politicians are on welfare?

Betty comes downstage, miming a shopping cart.

LISH:

How you doin', Betty?

BETTY:

Keeping myself between the ditches.

LUCY:

There was one lady in the block that was well and truly crazy.

Betty mimes taking some pills.

LUCY:

She had to take about seventeen pills a day to keep herself "between the ditches," like she said. She used to have a family and was working on a master's degree. What was your thesis on, Betty?

BETTY:

Critical Semiotics of South Amercian Magical Realism.

LUCY:

Just goes to show. We're all one chemical away from being crazy.

BETTY:

And how are you girls doing?

LISH:

Just fine, Betty. How about you?

BETTY:

I got some exciting news.

LISH:

And what's that, Betty?

BETTY:

I'm getting married!

LISH:

Really?

LUCY:

The kids around here used Betty as the ultimate insult.

Quick lighting shift. Lish becomes a kid, running around Betty, who has moved her scarf down to become Other Kid.

KID:

You love Betty! You love Betty!

OTHER KID:

TAKE IT BACK!

Lights return to normal and the scarf comes back up. The scene is reset.

LUCY:

So I wondered who was going to marry her around here, where there were single women everywhere you looked.

BETTY:

He's in prison in Baltimore.

LUCY:

There you go.

BETTY:

For murdering a woman.

LUCY:

There you go.

BETTY:

I'm gonna hitchhike down there and we're gonna get married.

LISH:

But Betty, how did he kill her? Was it like an accident or did he chop her up into little bits?

LUCY:

There's a big difference there.

LISH:

Yeah. If it's little bits, you should maybe...reconsider.

BETTY:

Tell you what, girls: If it's little bits, we'll just live together.

LUCY:

And then Betty showed us the dress she was gonna wear for the wedding, and it was totally beautiful.

Betty reaches into the laundry basket, pulling out a white blanket with lacy details. She holds it up to herself like a dress. She dances off.

LUCY:

I thought, for a nutbar, she had really good taste. And a couple of days after that, she was gone.

Betty flutters the blanket behind the scrim and disappears.

LUCY:

I don't know if she went to Baltimore or what, but I like to think she did. People do usually what they want to do, whether or not it's good for them, and even if they have to make up a good reason. Or have one made up for them.

LISH:

Lucy, Betty just gave me an idea.

LUCY:

Cruising prisons for men?

LISH:

Let's go to Denver. Let's find him.

LUCY:

Who?

LISH:

Gotcha.

LUCY:

No!

LISH:

Oh, Lucy, let's do it! Let's find him! It might be easy! He's on his way to Denver right now. We can head him off. If we miss him, we can ask around and maybe catch him at the next town.

LUCY:

Oh, I don't know, Lish.

LISH:

I have to do something. It's been like twenty letters now—

LUCY:

I got carried away—

LISH:

And he can't get into Canada on account of a drug bust.

LUCY:

I thought that was a nice touch—

LISH:

I got nothing to lose, and he's not that far away. Let's go and find him!

LUCY:

I don't know.

LISH:

C'mon, Lucy, I thought you would be excited! Even if nothing happens, at least we'd get out of Half-a-Life for a while.

LUCY:

It's just—

LISH:

Here, let me at least read you his last postcard—

Gotcha appears behind the scrim, centre.

GOTCHA:

Hey, Baby. You know, the more I think about you the more I regret ever leaving you. I'll be in the middle of my show and a picture of you will come to me and I'll forget the next bit. I've been doing the same schtick for years and I'll forget. We were only together for a short time but what we had was amazing. I keep having a dream that I look up from my juggling hands and see you there, smiling at me. Isn't that crazy? The festival got rained out in Detroit so I'm on my way to Denver. Maybe I'll have better luck there. I think of you every day, and at night I sleep with your wallet. All my love, GOTCHA.

LUCY:

I got *really* carried away.

LISH:

I mean he is practically inviting me there.

LUCY:

But Lish—

LISH:

I know! I know it's crazy. I know it's stupid and impractical and chances are nothing'll come of it. I know all that. But I have to try. You'll come with me, won't you, Lucy?

LUCY:

My mom told me there were only two things I should never do. She said I should never lie and I should never throw stones.

LISH:

You'll come with me, right?

LUCY:

I know I've thrown some stones since then, and now—

LISH:

You have to. You're my best friend.

LUCY:

I didn't know what to do.

LISH:

Please?

LUCY:

(*hugs her*)

LISH:

(*hugs her back*) Thank you! It will be so fun, you'll see! (*calling over to Rodger, exiting*) Rodger!

LUCY:

Lish made arrangements with Rodger down the way. We traded his van, which he lives in, for Lish's place, which will be empty. It was an easy sell, cause he was jonesing for some indoor plumbing.

Lish enters with the plunger. She sits at the table and is joined by Lucy. Lights narrow and it becomes the van.

LUCY:

Lish and me and Dill and Alba and Letitia, Maya and Hope. It's amazing we're here. There were lots of—what are those things that make it hard to do things?

LISH:

Obstacles.

LUCY:

Obstacles. One of the big ones is this— welfare mothers aren't allowed to just leave town. It's unfair to the taxpayers.

Lish exits, and Podborczintski enters, wearing his Rex Harrison hat. He sits at the table.

PODBORCZINTSKI:

Good morning, Lucy.

LUCY:

Morning, Mr. Podborczintski. (*out*) Now that I had my benefits going, I had a new welfare guy. He was way nicer. On one of my visits he said:

PODBORCZINTSKI:

We must make sure Dill knows, despite his random arrival into the world, that he is special, he is loved, and he is capable of making change, of creating beauty in his life, and in the lives around him.

LUCY:

I mean, is that inspiring or what? But on this particular day, he said something that freaked me out.

PODBORCZINTSKI:

I don't know if you're aware, Lucy, but we have to do a home visit. To accurately assess a client's needs and to make sure there is no…you understand.

LUCY:

A home visit?

PODBORCZINTSKI:

Yes. Sometime in the next while.

LUCY:

Oh. I see. (*out*) Big problem. If Podborczintski was planning a home visit, I would have to be home, not in Colorado, looking for an imaginary street performer. (*to him*) I wonder—can we arrange a specific time for an appointment? You see, because I'm outside a lot on account of I have lung problems and the rain is really good for them.

PODBORCZINTSKI:

I'm sorry, Lucy, the point of the visit is that it's a surprise. We need to know there is no…

LUCY:

Sure. (*nodding quickly*) He was sparing me suspicion, I was sparing him embarrassment.

PODBORCZINTSKI:

Take good care, then. I look forward to seeing your home.

They shake hands.

LUCY:

Me too.

Lucy moves downstage. Podborczintski takes off his hat and throws it up, behind the scrim. Lish enters with two plungers. She gives one to Podborczintski. They both lay on the floor, holding the handles under their arms, as if they have been stabbed with them.

LUCY:

You know that expression, gulping air? That's what I was doing when I got out of there. Gulping air. When I got back to Have-a-Life, Lish and all her kids were lying dead on the floor, having recently been brutally murdered. I think I handled it well:

Lights go red and Lucy screams, sobbingly.

LUCY:

AHHHHHHHHHHHHHHHHHHHHHHHHHHHHHHHHHHHHHHHHHHH!

Both Lish and Letitia bolt up, startled.

LISH:

Oh, Lucy, just kidding, just kidding. You see, Dill sleeps with his eyes a little bit open, and it gave the girls the idea— oh, Lucy.

LUCY:

That's not funny. Murder's not funny.

LISH:

I'm sorry, Luce. Look, it's just food coloring.

LETITIA:

Don't be sad, Lucy. See? We are perfectly alive. (*she waves her arms and legs to demonstrate how alive she is*)

LUCY:

Murder is not funny. You have just one murder in the family and it stops being funny forever.

LISH:

I'm really sorry.

Letitia exits, crying. Lish follows her.

LUCY:

(*slumps to a sit*) And right then I wondered just what the hell I was doing. How could I be Dill's mother and not know a damn thing about a damn thing? How could I expect to go to Colorado? How were our lives ever going to be funny and lucky? How was Dill ever going to be a man who is good and kind and strong? It just didn't seem possible at all.

Lish re-enters.

LISH:

I'm really sorry.

LUCY:

I'm scared, Lish.

LISH:

I know. It's okay.

LUCY:

How can we leave? I mean, it's all so hard, and I have a home visit coming up.

LISH:

It's difficult.

LUCY:

I mean we have the van and all, and that's good.

LISH:

Sure.

LUCY:

But we have to put gas in the van and eat food and everything.

LISH:

I know.

LUCY:

And I don't have any money saved up anywhere.

LISH:

Me neither.

LUCY:

And it'll take some money.

LISH:

Like five hundred dollars.

LUCY:

Really?

LISH:

I figure.

LUCY:

That's, like, astronomical.

LISH:

I know.

LUCY:

Where are we gonna get five hundred dollars?

LISH:

I'm gonna have to ask my dad.

LUCY:

Yeah?

LISH:

Yeah.

LUCY:

Oh.

LISH:

Yeah. And you have to come.

LUCY:

I do?

LISH:

Pack your infant, Lucy. We're going to the Four Seasons Hotel.

LUCY:

Why don't you just call him?

LISH:

I have to ask him in person.

LUCY:

Why not go over when he's at home?

LISH:

I have to ask him in public.

LUCY:

Oh.

LISH:

Yeah.

Lish exits.

LUCY:

Lish's parents were really well off. Lish had one of those great upbringings where the mom stays at home full-time and the dad works super hard and even helps around the house. And then Lish gets knocked up and becomes a welfare mom anyway. Just goes to show. Lish would tell us the story of how her parents met. It was one of the kids' favorites.

Lish and Letitia enter with teddy bears, which represent Grandma and Grandpa. They join Lucy by the toy box for story time. During this, the Fisher-Price house becomes the town, the trucks become puppets, the teddy bears become Lish's parents and all available props are brought in on the action.

LISH:

Grandma and Grandpa were from a small farming town, and in that town, there was a feud. A long and bitter feud that split the town right down the middle.

A ribbon appears from the box and lands on the Fisher Price house, splitting it down the middle.

LISH:

On one side were people who use John Deere Farm Equipment.

LETITIA:

(*puppeting her dump truck*) John Deere!

LISH:

On the other side were people who used Massey Ferguson farm equipment.

LUCY:

(*with her toy minivan*) Massey Ferguson!

LISH:

They took it very seriously. If one of their tractors broke down, they would fix it in the middle of the night, so the other side wouldn't see.

Lish pulls out a teddy bear with a removable arm.

LISH:

And if one of them lost an arm (*tearing off the arm*) due to a defective combine, the other side gloated about it for months and months.

Lucy's minivan laughs and laughs.

LISH:

(*pulling out a frog puppet*) When new families moved in, they had to decide very carefully which side to choose—

Letitia and Lucy each grab an arm of the puppet, pulling it back and forth between the two sides.

LISH:

—because the two sides hated each other, and once you chose, you were in for life.

Lights shift and Lish stands. Letitia crosses to the stage left stepladder to become the Hotel Guy.

LUCY:

The Four Seasons Hotel.

LISH:

Here we go.

LUCY:

We marched right in. This hotel was, like, super fancy. Lish acted real confident, but we looked like refugees. We were soaking wet from the walk over and had five kids between us. But Lish marched up to the front desk.

LISH:

Excuse me. I am attending the conference on security measures in North American banking. Which ballroom is that to be held in, please?

HOTEL GUY:

The Oak Room.

LISH:

Thank you.

HOTEL GUY:

But it is a private function.

LISH:

I should hope so. Riff-raff can be so displeasing.

HOTEL GUY:

You are a member of the convention?

LISH:

Yes, I am. I have to give the dreariest talk on internet encryption and Vocal DNA delivery.

HOTEL GUY:

But your children?

LISH:

Yes, I know. I couldn't get a sitter. But they come to every Kids at Work day and they are fantastically behaved.

LUCY:

Right then Alba had both her hands in her crotch because she had to pee and Letitia was climbing one of the fake trees in the lobby.

HOTEL GUY:

But—

LISH:

Alba, take your hands from your vagina.

HOTEL GUY:

Listen—

LISH:

I'm sorry, where was I going again?

HOTEL GUY:

The Oak Room.

LISH:

Thanks ever-so.

LUCY:

And we were in. Lish makes people believe her. It's her special talent.

Hotel Guy turns upstage and pulls Dad's glasses out of his pocket. He puts them on and turns downstage as Dad.

DAD:

Lucy, stop. Look down.

LUCY:

My dad had a special talent too.

DAD:

Do you see it?

LUCY:

He could look at a huge field of clover and immediately find a four-leaf one.

DAD:

Do you see it?

LUCY:

Yeah, Daddy. Should we pick it and get the luck?

DAD:

No. If you leave it there, the whole world's a little luckier. And that's better, right?

LUCY:

I guess so. (*out*) He would never pick them. He just noticed them and left them there. I told the kids at school about my dad's talent, but they weren't impressed. Another kid said—

Kid appears behind the scrim, centre.

KID:

My dad can fart the alphabet.

LUCY:

And they were impressed with that. So I told them my dad was the only baby in the world born wearing a little grey suit. I overheard my mom say that to a friend of hers on the phone, and it sounded very unique to me. But they weren't impressed with that either. My teacher asked me to sit down.

DAD:

There's another one. Can you see it, over there?

LUCY:

Dad was human when he was outside the house. He talked and relaxed and was normal. Inside the house he just went silent. I never knew what to say. I wondered if Lish's dad was like that.

Dad moves away upstage. He switches his glasses for those of Lish's Dad. Ballroom music floats in. We are back at the Four Seasons.

LISH:

Girls, go find your grandpa!

LETITIA:

Grandpa! Grandpa! Grandpa!

LUCY:

They all ran over to this distinguished-looking man and reached up for a cuddle.

Alba cuddles Lish's Dad.

LISH'S DAD:

Oh, my God.

Lish's Dad turns to excuse himself as Alba turns into Lish.

LUCY:
Lish's dad had a look on his face like we had just pulled down his pants and painted his ass blue.

LISH'S DAD:
Alicia! What are you doing here?

LUCY:
No, actually he looked more embarrassed than that.

LISH:
(*a little loudly*) Hi, Daddy.

LISH'S DAD:
(*fake-happily*) Alicia! (*he takes her arm and leads her across the stage to the toy box, angrily*) Alicia, what are you doing? This is completely inappropriate!

LISH:
I need some money, Daddy.

LISH'S DAD:
Money?

LISH:
And I'm not leaving until I get it.

LUCY:
Oh, my God. What is she doing?

The cast drops to the toy box, seamlessly rejoining their story in progress.

LISH:
So— There's Grandma and Grandpa, growing up in this town with this silly farm equipment feud. And I probably don't even have to tell you, Grandma was from a John Deere family and Grandpa was from a Massey Ferguson family. Neither of them gave a damn about farm equipment, so they went ahead and fell in love, even though it was a dangerous thing to do. When Great-Grandpa found out about the courtship he said:

Letitia puppets her dump truck as Great-grandpa.

GREAT-GRANDPA:
I forbid you to see that boy.

LISH:

But Grandma said: (*turns to Grandpa*) I love him! I love him more than I ever loved any John Deere plow! We are getting married and when we have a baby I am going to name it MASSEY FERGUSON!

GREAT-GRANDPA:

Aargh!

LISH:

And Grandma took off. On her way out of the driveway she took off her panties and flung them up onto a John Deere hauler.

Takes the panties off her teddy bear and throws them up.

LISH:

Then she mooned all the pigs and all the farm and all the John Deere equipment and went off with her man to start a new life. They were rebels in love. But they got older, and richer—

Lucy and Letitia slump the teddies over like they are old. Letitia puts Lish's Dad's glasses on the bear.

LISH:

—and as they got richer, they began to have a lot of respect for the rules. Whatever rebel they had left, they passed on to their daughter.

Lish pulls out a teddy bear that wears her signature beret.

ALL:

Yay!

They all stand up cheering, moving into position. Lights shift and we find Lish nose to nose with her father, just as we left them.

LISH'S DAD:

What exactly are you doing, Alicia?

LISH:

I'm extorting money from you, Daddy. I need a thousand dollars.

LUCY:

Lish's dad didn't know what to do. I felt a little bad for the guy. But him being so ashamed of her was the only weapon Lish had, and she figured since he was small-minded enough to be ashamed, he deserved what he got.

LISH'S DAD:

This is disgraceful, Alicia. I have never been so embarrassed.

LISH:

I know, Daddy. I'm very embarrassing. Do you want to write a cheque now, or should I mingle for a while and come back?

Lish moves into the party, threateningly. Lish's Dad whispers urgently after her.

LISH'S DAD:

A thousand dollars?

LISH:

...Fifteen hundred.

Lish's Dad angrily writes a cheque.

LUCY:

I couldn't believe it. That's Lish's other special talent. She doesn't care if people like her or not. Not even her own father. I think that's amazing. I don't know if my father likes me or not, but I'd do just about anything to make sure he did. I think most people are like me.

LISH'S DAD:

Here.

LISH:

Thanks, Daddy.

LISH'S DAD:

Now get out of here before your mother sees you.

LISH:

I love you.

LISH'S DAD:

That makes one of us.

Lish's Dad exits quickly behind the scrim. He trades glasses and bends over, arms outstretched, into the light. Only his torso is lit. It looks as if he is flying.

LUCY:

When I was a kid in school, I wrote a story about my dad. I wrote that he could fly and lift a car and drink the ocean and do hard math, all in his head. I guess kids can't help writing their wish-parents, just like parents can't help writing the stories of their kids, before they even find out who they are. How do you avoid being disappointed?

Lights out on Dad.

LISH:

Did you see the look on his face?

LUCY:

Wow, Lish. Holy cow.

LISH:

I nailed him!

LUCY:

I've never seen anything like that!

LISH:

He oughta know better than to mess with me!

LUCY:

I know! It was amazing, Lish, I— Then I noticed Lish wasn't laughing. She was crying.

LISH:

He hates me. He just hates me.

LUCY:

Ah, Lish.

LISH:

Well, fuck him, that's what I say. Fuck him.

LUCY:

Oh, sweetie. (*hugs her*) I guess Lish does care what her father thinks of her. I know I do, and I barely know mine. And looking at poor Dill, he's not gonna know his at all. I worry about that. About Dill not knowing his father. I worry that he'll feel robbed.

John Dillinger appears behind the scrim, centre. He brandishes a super soaker water gun.

DILLINGER:

Now lie down on the floor and nobody gets hurt.

Everyone gets on the floor. Lucy continues her story from there. Dillinger moves downstage, menacing the audience with his large water gun.

LUCY:

I named Dill for John Dillinger, because I want him to have that outlaw spark, but without all the crime and that. Dillinger didn't kill anyone. He just robbed banks. Good for him, I say. Stupid banks.

Dillinger puts his gun up. Lish has put on a hat and grabbed a super soaker of her own. She is now J. Edgar Hoover.

DILLINGER:

Stay calm, ladies and gents. This won't take but a moment.

SFX: Machine gun fire. J. Edgar shoots Dillinger, who falls in a heap.

LUCY:

J. Edgar Hoover shot Dillinger, or that's what they say. Some people think he's still alive, and that's what I think too.

Dillinger stands up and smiles. J. Edgar becomes his girlfriend, standing flirtily.

LUCY:

I think his girlfriend set up somebody else. Here's why. You see, John Dillinger had this tremendous penis. Over twelve inches—

Dillinger pulls out the plunger of his super soaker to represent his endowment.

LUCY:

—and the guy J. Edgar shot had what I would call merely a big dick, at nine inches.

Dillinger's girlfriend has a smaller super soaker. Dillinger is dismissive.

LUCY:

Even still, it's in a jar at the Smithsonian. But I think the real John Dillinger's dick is still out there, attached to its owner.

GIRLFRIEND:

You betta believe it.

LUCY:

I think him and his girlfriend ran off somewhere and lived happily ever after.

Dillinger and his girlfriend move to exit, then they turn suddenly, spraying the audience liberally as they leave.

LUCY:

I like to think of Mom that way too. Maybe someday she'll show up with airplane tickets and whisk me and Dill to South America or somewhere. She would love Dill. She loved babies.

Mom appears, behind the scrim, right

MOM:

Look at you.You precious thing.You're a precious, precious thing.

Mom looks out at Lucy. She comes from around the screen, moves to Lucy and hugs her.

LUCY:

But I don't think that'll really happen.That's just a dream everybody has when somebody dies.

They turn in the hug and become Lucy and Lish again.

LISH:

I'm okay now.

LUCY:

Yeah?

LISH:

It just gets me, you know?

LUCY:

Sure.

LISH:

Did you hear him?

LUCY:

He was just mad.

LISH:

Yeah.

LUCY:

Yeah.

LISH:

Serves him right.

LUCY:

Yeah.

LISH:

That's not even a lot of money for them. That's like the bottled water budget.

LUCY:

Yeah. It's okay to steal from rich people. Especially if they're mean.

LISH:

You think?

LUCY:

You're an outlaw, Lish. I love outlaws.

LISH:

(*makes guns with her hands*) Gimme all your money and nobody gets hurt.

Lucy puts up her hands.

LISH:

'Night.

LUCY:

'Night.

LISH:

We're going to Colorado!

LUCY:

Okay!

LUCY:

And I went inside and I checked the answering machine. My dad got it for me.

SFX: Beep. Dad appears behind the scrim, left.

DAD:

Uh, hello, Lucy. This is your father speaking.

LUCY:

I think he calls when I'm out on purpose. He's shy.

DAD:

Just wanted to say that I am at home and I'm well, and uh… I hope you are well, too. I hope you are well very much… Goodnight.

Lights down on Dad.

LUCY:

'Night, Dad. I hope you are well too. I hope you are well very much.

Fade to black.

End of Act One

Act Two

Lucy and Lish are in the van. They sit a moment in silence. Lucy laughs softly to herself.

LISH:
What are you thinking about?

LUCY:
What?

LISH:
Are you thinking about that guy?

LUCY:
Hmm?

LISH:
The guy you left the party with.

LUCY:
Oh, he just gave me a ride home.

LISH:
You are a lying liar.

LUCY:
He gave me a ride home.

LISH:
And what did you give him?

Lish masturbates the stickshift.

LUCY:
Frankly, I am shocked at what you're suggesting. (*turns to the audience*) I met a guy at the party, and it'll be another twenty miles before Lish pulls it out of me. Oh, yeah, we went to a party. But not just for fun. As a preparation for our trip. Lish said—

Lighting change. They step off the table into Lish's kitchen.

LISH:
Do you want to meet Graham Greene?

LUCY:
What?

LISH:

Do you want to meet Graham Greene? The actor.

LUCY:

Uh, sure. Is he in your purse?

LISH:

He's gonna be at the party.

LUCY:

The party?

LISH:

We have to go to this party. It's a film wrap party. To prepare for our trip.

LUCY:

What are you talking about?

LISH:

It's all about levels.

LUCY:

Levels.

LISH:

Sure. See, your fun levels are very low right now. And it's affecting your courage levels.

LUCY:

Yeah?

LISH:

Oh, yeah. Fun levels are directly tied to courage levels. And we need our courage levels high, because adventures are scary. So we need to have some fun, recover our courage, so we can believe in our adventure.

LUCY:

We do?

LISH:

Yeah. Without the fun, an adventure won't be believable to us, because we never have any fun. Understand?

LUCY:

No.

LISH:

You don't have to. You just have to come to this party.

LUCY:

But I don't—

LISH:

C'mon! Don't you want to Dance with Wolves? Don't you want to Run Brave? Don't you want to Die Hard 3?

LUCY:

I guess.

LISH:

Great. Then we're going to this party.

LUCY:

So Sing Dylan was going to take care of the kids. It was a rare chance to be ignored by a famous person. We took the kids over.

Sing comes around the corner of the scrim.

SING:

Hello to you and your beautiful children!

LISH:

Hey, Mr. Tambourine Man.

LUCY:

Thanks, Sing.

SING:

Thanks are not necessary. It is good practice for me to take of babies. It is I who thank you. Thank you kindly.

LUCY:

You're totally welcome.

LISH:

See ya!

Sing chases the kids in.

SING:

(*heard off*) Please put down my statue of Vishnu!

Lish turns to Lucy.

LISH:

Lucy, do you know what he meant by that?

LUCY:

Not really.

LISH:

Has Sarah gained weight?

LUCY:

She looks happy. (*out*) Emmanual was visiting more often now, and when he left they smiled instead of crying.

LISH:

Is she glowing?

LUCY:

(*shrugging*) Soon we were up to our ankles in discarded outfits.

They take a white blanket and cover themselves in it, as if they are changing clothes under it.

LUCY:

Lish finally settled on the big green sweater and black tights, with all fifteen bracelets and the red rubber boots.

Lish whips off the blanket. She is dressed the same.

LUCY:

Nice.

LISH:

Thanks.

LUCY:

I went with the classic tight jeans and a black T-shirt. I was putting on my lipstick when Lish started to cry.

LISH:

BWAH AH AHHHH AHHHHHHH.

LUCY:

Oh, my God, what's wrong?

LISH:

Nothing. I just like how I look after I cry. My lips get nice and puffy and my eyes sort of shine. It only takes like five minutes.

LUCY:

Yeah?

LISH:

Yeah. (*resumes sobbing*)

LUCY:

And I watched her cry, and I wondered what she was thinking about to cry like that, and then I thought about my mother and poor fatherless Dill, and my own father and the home…visit…(*tearing up*) and then I—pretty soon I was cry—cry—BWAH AHHHHH…

They cry for a long time. Lish checks her watch.

LISH:

(*sobbing*) Keep it going, keep it going.

They gradually stop and then wipe some tears away and look at each other.

LISH:

You look great.

LUCY:

You too.

LISH:

Party time!

SFX and LX: Party Atmosphere. Lish dances with men behind the scrim.

LUCY:

Lish shone at the party. She knew how to talk to men so that they talked back. These were different men than Sing or Joe. They wore V-neck sweaters in pastel colors and drank beer from glasses. And I think we were a novel change for them too. We weren't the marrying sort, probably not even good enough for dating, but some harmless flirtation, even sex, might be a nice break away from their own lives.

Lish comes around the corner, talking to a man.

LISH:

And that's how sociology is different from anthropology.

MAN:

(*muttering*) Wow, that's amazing…

The man turns quickly and becomes Graham Greene.

LUCY:

She was amazing. She got to meet Graham Greene.

GRAHAM GREENE:

Hello there.

Lish grabs Graham Greene's ass.

GRAHAM GREENE:

Oh!

LUCY:

Graham Greene didn't talk to me. But a lawyer did.

Graham Greene turns and becomes Hartley. Lish exits.

HART:

(*holding out his hand*) Hartley Weinstein.

LUCY:

He didn't talk to his other friends or colleagues; he just talked to me. It would have been faster if he said:

HART:

I was hoping we could have sex.

LUCY:

Since that was obviously what he wanted. But he smelled nice, and was sort preppy cute.

HART:

You seem too young to have a kid.

LUCY:

I totally am.

HART:

Still, I'm sure you're a great mother and all.

LUCY:

Oh, yeah.

HART:

Sure.

LUCY:

You seem too young to be a lawyer.

HART:

I sort of am.

LUCY:

So he's trying to impress me. He's like the Doogie Hawser of lawyering.

HART:

I skipped grade two.

LUCY:

Cool. And I felt sorry for his wife. I was sure he must have one. But then I felt mean. I thought of all those women who look at us with our kids and Safeway bags and substandard strollers and lack of men and cars. Then I thought maybe I would have sex with her husband, just for revenge. Then I thought I would have four more beers to help decide. And then while we were dancing I said:

You know what I need?

HART:

What's that?

LUCY:

A ride home.

HART:

I can do that.

LUCY:

Yeah?

HART:

I only had two beers.

LUCY:

Okay then.

Hartley moves to the toy box and sits on it. He grabs the minivan and holds it in front of him.

LUCY:

Then I suddenly felt sad, because all I really wanted was a boyfriend my own age, with long hair, and wiry arms. This is what I was thinking when I got into Hart's Ford Aerostar.

Hartley moves a Lego block from the front seat of the minivan and into the back of it.

LUCY:

He moved a car seat out of the front, thinking I was too drunk to notice.

Hart gestures and Lucy sits on the toy box beside him.

HART:

Here we go.

They bounce a little on the toy box as if driving.

LUCY:

Here we are.

HART:

Wow. That was fast.

LUCY:

When he got to my place he took off his shoes. Then he stepped on one hard block and then another.

Hart steps on some Lego left out on the floor.

HART:

Ow...ow.

LUCY:

I couldn't stop laughing.

HART:

You're crazy, aren't you?

LUCY:

Sometimes.

HART:

(*looking around*) Crazy.

LUCY:

And I knew he wanted me to be crazy. Making up for poverty with a *joie de vivre*, a skid row toughness all softened on top by a layer of tenderness. You know, Hollywood. I moved all the toys off the bed and we got in.

They sit on the kitchen table. They hold a blanket up to their chins, making a bed.

HART:

You hot little tomato, you.

LUCY:

He called me a tomato. That's not alluring. Produce is not alluring.

HART:

You're so beautiful.

LUCY:

Better. And then he started into his foreplay routine. All by the book.

Lucy holds the blanket and Hart disappears under it. A sex instructor appears behind the scrim, left. She speaks in a German accent.

INSTRUCTOR:

First attend to the lower half of the woman. Then move up to the upper half, maintaining pressure on the lower. When all dash lights are on, you may encourage the woman to take hold of the stick shift.

LUCY:

I started to envy his wife. She was being spared all this.

Hart pokes his head above the blanket.

HART:

You hot red pepper, you!

LUCY:

And then Hart grabbed one of my breasts and sucked it hard.

HART:

(*jumping up*) OH, MY GOD! What the hell was— Oh, my God, it got right in my mouth!

LUCY:

(*out*) Oh, yeah.

HART:

Oh, my good Jesus God— what was that?

LUCY:

(*laughing*)

HART:

Oh, God. Oh, my God.

LUCY:

Calm down, Hartley. It's perfectly natural.

HART:

Natural? To have liquid leaking out of your—!

LUCY:

Yes.

Pause.

HART:

Oh. Oh. That's— Right…That was—that was milk, wasn't it?

LUCY:

Yeah, Hart. I have a baby. I breast-feed him.

HART:

People still do that?

LUCY:

Yeah.

HART:

You must think I'm an idiot.

LUCY:

No. Well…no.

Pause.

LUCY:

Well… You probably have to get home, right? I think I see the sun coming up.

HART:

You want me to go?

LUCY:

Don't you like, have to?

HART:

It's okay. My mom's in Florida.

LUCY:

What?

HART:

She won't know what time I get in.

LUCY:

You live with your mom?

HART:

Well, yeah, right now.

LUCY:

What about the car seat in the minivan?

HART:

It's my brother's. I have this '69 Mustang, but it's in the shop. It's always in the shop.

LUCY:

Oh.

HART:

Yeah.

LUCY:

A Mustang?

HART:

Yeah. Listen, do you want to…see me?

LUCY:

I can see you, Hart. You're standing right here.

HART:

I mean, see me again sometime. Like a date.

LUCY:

Oh—um—maybe. Right before my eyes he turned from a cheating asshole slumming with a welfare case—

Hart becomes an ogre, rubbing his hands lasciviously.

LUCY:

—to an actual sort of cute guy.

Hart turns and makes cute-guy faces at the audience.

LUCY:

It was very confusing. So I did what I always did when a man confused me. (*to Hart*) Would you like some coffee?

HART:

Sure.

They settle into the kitchen chairs.

LUCY:

So tell me about yourself.

HART:

Uh, okay. I—

Hart goes through the motions as if he is telling Lucy all the things mentioned. Sounds float in supportively, the saxophone, a crazy lady, the American national anthem.

LUCY:

And he told me about how he wanted to be a saxophone player instead of a lawyer and how his ex-girlfriend went crazy and how his brother sells junk bonds and how his parents were divorced and his mom was dating an American. I showed him a picture of Dill and he said:

HART:

He looks like you.

LUCY:

And right then I looked at him. And his hair wasn't all that short. And his arms were kind of wiry.

Knock, knock, knock. Lish holds the Podborczintski hat out from behind the scrim.

LUCY:

Then the door knocked. I figured it was Sing to return Dill.

Hart runs over to beneath the hat. He plays Podborczintski for a moment.

LUCY:

But I looked out the peephole and it was Podborczintski.

Hart runs back and is Hart again. Knock, knock, knock!

LUCY:

Oh, no. You have to get out of here.

HART:

Why?

LUCY:

It's my welfare guy and you are not supposed to be here.

HART:

Why?

LUCY:

I can't have sex.

HART:
You can't?

LUCY:
It's unfair to the taxpayers.

HART:
But we didn't have sex.

LUCY:
You sucked my boob.

HART:
So?

LUCY:
That's a government boob!

HART:
Okay.

LUCY:
Okay!

HART:
Where do I go?

LUCY:
Over the balcony.

HART:
The balcony?

LUCY:
The balcony!

HART:
Over the balcony?

LUCY:
Yes! Right now!— And here was the moment where he could say—

HART:
That's ridiculous. I'm leaving.

LUCY:
And just walk out the front door and fuck my life up completely. But instead he said:

HART:

Okay. Let's go.

They use the chairs to ascend the kitchen table.

LUCY:

And we got up to balcony. He threw his shoes over. Do you want me to tie a sheet or something?

HART:

That doesn't work. I'll jump.

LUCY:

You'll kill yourself.

HART:

As if.

He kisses her dramatically, and then steps over the railing.

HART:

So maybe you can call me or some— AH!

He falls from the table, hurting his ankle. He gives a thumbs-up to Lucy and limps off.

LUCY:

And down he went. He was starting to resemble my fantasy boyfriend a bit now. Hmmm.

Lucy remembers herself and runs about cleaning up. Hart runs around behind the scrim and joins the Podborczintski hat. Lucy opens the door.

LUCY:

Mr. Podborczintski! How are you?

PODBORCZINTSKI:

Just fine, Lucy. How are you?

LUCY:

Okay. Come on in. And soon we were walking around looking at things. When we got to the bedroom I had to pounce on the pillow before Mr. Podborczintski saw it. Hart had left his business card there. Hartley Weinstein. Barrister and Solicitor. He may be a lawyer, but he does a fair impression of an outlaw.

Podborczintski whips off his hat and spins to become Hart. Wild west outlaw music plays. Hart shoots Lucy with his finger and she swoons. Lish comes around to sit on the table. Lights shift into the van.

LUCY:

And I was thinking about him. So there.

They drive silently for a moment

LUCY:

We were just a bit outside the city. We were driving past flooded houses and flooded farms and whole flooded towns.

LISH:

Look at that.

LUCY:

I know. It was a real natural disaster. Right here in Canada. I know it happens in other places all the time, but I never lived through one before. The whole city reacts. Everyone was helping out. Like Naomi.

Lighting shift. Lucy and Lish sit at the chairs in Lish's kitchen. Naomi comes around the corner, agitated.

NAOMI:

Hey, guys. Guess what's going on now with Bunnie BLEEP-ing Hutchinson?

LISH:

What?

Lish and Naomi freeze.

LUCY:

Naomi got a second job working for the flood disaster board. There were 16,000 flooded basements in town and the disaster board was hiring anybody with a pulse. Cattle were dying so often that farmers had started to kill themselves too. The army was around filling up sandbags. It seemed everyone was trying to help. Everyone except:

Naomi unfreezes.

NAOMI:

Bunnie BLEEP-ing Hutchinson.

She freezes again.

LUCY:

Here's Naomi's schedule.

Lish drops to her knees and becomes Tina. They go through a pantomime of their day as Lucy narrates.

LUCY:

Up at dawn with Tina to get her ready, get her to daycare—

TINA:

Bye.

LUCY:

—work all day, get Tina back—

TINA:

Hi!

LUCY:

—take her home on the bus, get dinner into her and collapse at 9:30, every single day. Being the working poor is super hard.

Naomi returns to her freeze, which looks quite angry.

LUCY:

No wonder she's angry all the time. Oh wait, there's another reason:

NAOMI:

Guess who filed for benefits down at the flood relief disaster board?

LISH:

Bunnie Hutchinson?

NAOMI:

Bunnie BLEEP-ing Hutchinson. See, Bunnie said on her form that she didn't have insurance and she need money for damage to lifting tiles and shifting foundations and loss of several fur coats and a big screen TV and the BLEEP-ing leather and the BLEEP-ing fridge from her mini-bar and a two-thousand-dollar aquarium that housed eight rare piranhas that were dead from the change in their BLEEP-ing climate.

LISH:

Piranhas?

NAOMI:

Yeah. BLEEP-ing piranhas. So I did the routine check of her city tax bill and get this. She *does* have insurance to cover flood sewage and other natural disasters.

So I think, gee, that's weird, there must be some mistake. So I show it to my supervisor and he's all, like—

Naomi spins and becomes the supervisor.

SUPERVISOR:

—Whoa, oh, hey, whoa now, I'll take that, hush hush, not a word now—

NAOMI:

—and all like that!

Lish and Naomi freeze.

LUCY:

I just thought Naomi was talking about her day and how even the government makes mistakes sometimes. But maybe there's more to it than that. 'Cause last week I watched Joe from down the way deliberately smash his car into a pole in the parking lot. He'd report it like a hit and run accident and collect the insurance so that him and Mercy could buy groceries. Then when they were flush Joe would get another beater for a hundred bucks or so. And I suddenly thought— That's what Bunnie Hutchinson is doing! She's running a scam! But not to buy groceries, to buy piranhas! Bunnie BLEEP-ing Hutchinson.

Lish and Naomi unfreeze to look shocked at Lucy. Naomi exits and Lish and Lucy reform the van. They look at all the flood's devastation.

LUCY:

For Pete's sake.

LISH:

All those poor farmers.

LUCY:

I know. (*out*) I wondered how many of them were also having divorces and the flu and a broken leg. When you add the natural disasters to the personal disasters, it makes you wonder how anybody can live at all.

LISH:

When it rains, it pours.

LUCY:

Things just stack up. Like how I looked up just then. Just in time— Wait— That sign.

LISH:

Fresh honey?

LUCY:

Stop the van.

LISH:

I don't think we can take honey over the border, Lucy.

LUCY:

My mom died under that sign.

LISH:

Really?

LUCY:

Stop the van!

LISH:

Stopping the van.

LUCY:

This was the sign. (*getting out*)

LISH:

Oh, my God.

LUCY:

This sign right here.

LISH:

Wow.

LUCY:

It's so faded now. All the paint's chipping off. It was brand new when Mom died. It was brand new. How long does that take, for a sign to get like that?

LISH:

I don't know.

LUCY:

How long has it been? We came out here, the cops took us out here, to see where she died. The cops were worried about Dad. He kept asking the farmer—

Dad appears behind the scrim, right.

DAD:

Do you sell a lot of honey? How much honey do you sell?

LUCY:

She dies every day in my head. But the sign is so faded. It feels like five minutes ago we got the phone call. But it's been years. And there's still so much I don't know. I don't know, like, when she got her first perm. And why did she want to be a therapist? Did she ever have an affair? And how, how did she get the scar on the back of her leg? Who can tell me? Who can tell me now?

Dad appears centre. Seated as if in a car.

DAD:

Slow down. You'll kill us all.

LUCY:

Mom would drive so fast. She had no fear of flying through the world, down her roads, going to new places at breakneck speed. And Dad was always a passenger.

Dad appears behind the scrim, left, as in the end of Act One.

DAD:

I am well...and I hope you are well too. I hope you are well very much.

LUCY:

When I was nine, my dad had painted a bench. I guess everyone was saying it was pink, so he asked me what colour it was. I said: (*switching to young Lucy*) Rose?

Dad appears behind the scrim, centre.

DAD:

Yes! Yes, it is! Good girl! Look at it. It's clearly rose.

LUCY:

And from then on I tried to make him happy and alive like that again. To get any reaction at all.

Dad comes around the corner of the scrim. Lucy breaks from the sign and speaks to him.

DAD:

Lucy? What are these suitcases?

LUCY:

I'm moving out, Dad. I'm pregnant. I'm pregnant and I don't know who the father is.

DAD:

I— I see. You're…expecting?

LUCY:

Yeah.

DAD:

And you don't know—

LUCY:

No.

DAD:

Well. I can't say I approve.

LUCY:

Okay.

DAD:

Do you need anything?

LUCY:

No.

Dad is crushed. He walks away.

LUCY:

And I wish I had said, Yes, Daddy. I need you.

Lights shift back to the side of the highway.

LUCY:

And right now I need him even more. Because he is the only one who knows what this honey sign means. The only person who misses my mom as much as I do. Maybe more. And I was filled with such a longing to see my dad. To hold his hand and tell him I knew how he felt. How had we lost track of each other for so long?

LISH:

Should we stay here for a while?

LUCY:

We should get to the border. I wanna call my dad.

LISH:

Okay.

LUCY:

Lish did the talking with the customs guy. He didn't quite know what to make of us, so I had some time to run to a pay phone.

Dad appears behind the scrim, left. He is watching his answering machine.

DAD:

(*voice-over*) Hello.You have reached the home of Jeffery Van Alstyne. I'm sorry, I am unable to answer the phone at this time. Please leave a message and I will call you as soon as I am able. Thank you. Here comes the beep.

Beep.

LUCY:

Uh, hi, Dad. It's Lucy. I'm calling from—

Dad hurriedly picks up the phone.

DAD:

Lucy?

LUCY:

Hi, Dad. Screening your calls?

DAD:

I'm just trying to avoid Mrs. Sawatsky.

LUCY:

Do you owe her money or something?

DAD:

No. She's determined to have me for dinner some night and I—

LUCY:

What, like a date? Geez.

DAD:

No, well, no. In any case, I have no intention, umm—

LUCY:

Peeling honey sign, my dad on a date? How long had it been anyway?

DAD:

How are you, Lucy?

LUCY:

Good. I'm calling from the border. Me and a friend are going on a little holiday.

DAD:

Do you have a reliable vehicle?

LUCY:

(*lying*) Oh, yeah.

DAD:

Good. Drive carefully.

LUCY:

Dad, I passed the honey sign.

DAD:

Oh. Yes.

LUCY:

I miss Mom.

DAD:

Well…of course…um…I also…well, it goes without saying.

LUCY:

Does it?

DAD:

I had assumed it did. I might be wrong.

Pause.

LUCY:

So, Dad—

DAD:

Yes?

LUCY:

Can we get together…sometime?

DAD:

Well, of course! I would like that! I'll come over when you get back!

LUCY:

Sure.. We can get a hamburger or something, or go for a walk.

DAD:

Yes, I'll come over…I um…I'm embarrassed to ask…

LUCY:

I gave Dad my address. He had never been there.

DAD:

I'll come over.

LUCY:

Yes.

DAD:

And see the place.

LUCY:

Yeah.

DAD:

Okay.

Pause.

DAD:

I appreciate you calling me.

LUCY:

You bet. I should probably get back in the van.

DAD:

All right then. No speeding, ha ha.

LUCY:

Okay, ha.

DAD:

Bye bye.

LUCY:

It was the longest conversation we ever had. And it went really good. Really good. Soon Dill will be walking and my father would've thought he'd always walked. He'd know, but he wouldn't, you know? You can't have that. You can't have people missing everything.

The border guard comes on, wearing aviator glasses. He speaks in an American accent.

GUARD:

Nature and purpose of the visit?

LUCY:

At welfare they always want to know who Dill's father was. Maybe next time I'll say, "Well, I know who my father is." Doesn't that count for something?

GUARD:

And what do you do in Winnipeg?

LISH:

I raise my kids.

GUARD:

All these children are yours?

LISH:

And hers.

LUCY:

Huh? Oh, hi! (*she waves*) I'm trying super hard to look normal. The guard looked at us a long time.

The Guard looks at Lish, closer, closer, until his nose is actually pressed up against her cheek.

LUCY:

Longer. Even longer than that. Yeah…about that long.

GUARD:

Enjoy your stay.

LUCY:

Thank you.

LISH:

Can you guarantee that we'll enjoy our stay? Because I would like—

LUCY:

Let's go, Lish.

LISH:

Okay. (*to the Guard*) I just want to say, we think America is just swell, and—

GUARD:

Move along.

LISH:

I'm trying. It's all I do.

They wave and start the van. The guard shuffles backwards as if the van is moving forward.

LUCY:

And off we went. Now that we were across the border, Lish was taking on a more serious look. Gotcha was close, she thought, and she was full of purpose. Waiting to see what would become of the juggler and her.

They pull out the blanket and lay on the table, as if it is the bed in the hotel.

LUCY:

That night we all piled into the cheapest motel we could find. The kids were asleep and breathing all around us, and me and Lish were like teenagers, staying up, talking about boys.

Lish sits up in bed.

LISH:

Lucy, do you think I'm stupid?

LUCY:

What do you mean?

LISH:

All this trouble looking for this guy.

LUCY:

You're not stupid.

LISH:

I mean, what am I gonna say to him?

LUCY:

I don't know.

LISH:

This is so crazy.

LUCY:

It's not crazy. It's funny. It's a funny thing to do, and we're lucky to be doing it.

LISH:

You're right. Maybe it'll be good.

LUCY:

Yeah.

LISH:

It is good already.

LUCY:

It is. I mean, even if you never find him or see him, or even if he didn't even exist, this would all be still good, right?

LISH:

Sure.

LUCY:

Sure, because life is in the journey, right? Like you always say, people are so hung up on results, right? It's stupid.

LISH:

Yeah. I know that and all.

LUCY:

Yeah?

LISH:

But I still hope I see him.

LUCY:

Right. But even if you don't, it's still good?

LISH:

Maybe.

Small pause.

LISH:

I've decided. It's good. 'Night, Lucy.

Lish lies back, leaving Lucy sitting up.

LUCY:

'Night.

LISH:

(starts to snore)

LUCY:

I was treating Lish's life like a Brazilian soap opera. What will happen next? We can't keep looking for Gotcha. I mean, what if we find him? I had to get rid of him, the sooner the better. I had to kill him. I had a plan. I call it "The Death of Gotcha." It's the biggest lie yet, but I don't know what else to do. I wrote the postcard and mailed it before we left Winnipeg. It's probably in a bag just waiting to go into our little tin mailbox all the way back in Canada. In a few days we'll call and ask about the mail. And Naomi will read a postcard from one of Gotcha's friends. And it will say:

Gotcha's Friend appears behind the scrim, left.

GOTCHA'S FRIEND:

I don't know how to tell you this, Lish, but Gotcha is dead. It was a drive-by shooting, a gang thing, and they got him by accident, outside of a movie theatre.

LUCY:

Just like John Dillinger. And it would also say:

GOTCHA'S FRIEND:

Gotcha never forgot you, Lish. He talked about you right up to the day he died. He said that he would never forget your long black hair and your laugh and the fun you guys had. He always regretted stealing your wallet and he was glad that you had the silver spoon as a token of his love. He also said that he loved kids and always wanted one of his own. Maybe two.

LUCY:

And wasn't that better? To know that he loved her and died dramatically?

GOTCHA'S FRIEND:

Anyway, he's gone now. Gone completely and forever, where no one can find him. But I'll never forget him. Just like he never forgot you. And now I will honour him in the way of our people:

Gotcha's Friend bends over and lights a flashpaper fart, then looks out sadly.

LUCY:

Better a late father than an absent one. Right, Lish?

Lish talks in her sleep.

LISH:

Stop it, people can see us…

LUCY:

I thought of my own father. Better a father late than a father never… Maybe I could have a late father yet, and all while he's still alive?

LISH:

SSSSSNNNNNNNNOOOOOOORE!

LUCY:

Lish snores like a wildebeest. I bet you didn't know that. Lish, you snore like a wildebeest!

LISH:

(*sleepily cheerful*) Oh, thank you very much.

LUCY:

And before I slept, I said a little prayer.

Lucy gets out of bed and kneels beside it.

LUCY:

That me and Lish would laugh about this one day. That she would be happy. That I would be happy. That life would be funny. That Dill was a lucky boy, father or no. Please?

Lights dip to black. When they come up, Lucy and Lish are back in the van. Letitia runs on and sits on the table behind them. Lish drives determinedly.

LUCY:

Denver was getting closer and closer. If we get there, the whole thing's done, and I don't have a best friend or a life, or a ride back to Canada. I started to talk a lot about mail. Mail this and mail that, and isn't it neat how the mail works? And I wonder, Lish, if you got any mail? And Lish finally decided to pull over.

Lish pulls the van over and gets out. She picks up a toy phone from the laundry basket and speaks into it.

LUCY:

I could only hear one side of the conversation.

LISH:

What?

No way.

Yeah, read it to me.

Jesus.

No.

No.

Oh, my God.

Did you say silver spoon?

Thanks. I'm sorry too.

How do you like them apples?

Yeah.

Yes.

What? Yeah, it's still running.

Yeah, I'll still get your smokes.

'Kay.

Bye.

LUCY:

And there it was. He was dead.

Lish gets back into the van. She drives silently for a moment and then explodes.

LISH:

DAMN IT! DAMMIT. DAMN THAT...THAT STUPID STUPID ASSHOLE. I was almost there.

LUCY:

And the girls wanted to know what had happened.

Letitia pops her head up.

LISH:

The person we were trying to find was killed in a terrible stupid accident and we are going home now.

LUCY:

And everybody got very quiet. Even Dill seemed to have respect for the situation. Lish was driving and crying, and after she'd cried, I'd say, "You look great," because she really did. And other than that I just said: "I'm sorry."

LISH:

It's not your fault.

LUCY:

Even though it was, it so was, and who the hell did I think I was? If I wanted to fix somebody's life so badly why hadn't I started with my own? I kept apologizing and apologizing.

LISH:

It's not your fault.

LUCY:

I encouraged you to take the trip.

LISH:

It's not your fault.

LUCY:

It was doomed from the start.

LISH:

It's not your fault.

LUCY:

I set up the whole thing and wrote all the letters and then killed Gotcha.

LISH:

What?

LUCY:

Except I didn't say the last part. I said everything but that.

LISH:

Shut up and stop blaming yourself. Women always apologize when it rains at a picnic.

LUCY:

And then she drove for a long time without saying anything. Just thinking. I could see her thinking. She drove and drove, her big hairy leg up on the dash board. This had gone all wrong. There was no payoff. No benefit to the end of wondering. Just sadness and pain and more pain and grief. And just then, like the punchline of a joke, the sun started to shine.

LISH:

Look at that.

LUCY:

The big prairie sun was doing what it's famous for. Being big and hot and red.

LISH:

I guess it wasn't meant to be.

LUCY:

And I felt a shift in Lish. Like a decision settling.

LISH:

Well, if the sun can shine again, maybe I can too. Huh, Lucy? Girls? What do you think?

LETITIA:

Sure, Mommy! Be shiny!

LISH:

Okay, Baby. I'll be shiny.

LUCY:

And she fell silent again. But I could see a little smile. I could see her bobbing her head to the music. I could see Lish. She was back.

Lish smiles at Lucy. "Here comes the Sun" plays out. Dip to black. The company flies into action to create the tent. A sheet comes from the laundry basket and is thrown over the table. Two plungers on the table become the tentpoles, and the illusion is complete. Letitia exits, and a lighter sparks in the darkness.

LISH:

How did the pioneers do it?

LUCY:

We had decided to camp. We were short on funds and we found a pretty lake. Lish was trying to light a fire, using bourbon as lighter fluid.

LISH:

Screw this. Let's go skinny-dipping.

LUCY:

And so we did.

They mime undressing and go behind the scrim. The lights become watery.

LUCY:

Two women and five kids, stark naked in a lake. We're naked right now. In front of all you people.

The Ranger enters, denoted by his ranger hat. He is shy.

RANGER:

Ahem.

LUCY:

And then a park ranger showed up.

RANGER:

Excuse me—

LUCY:

I tried to keep my breasts under the water without drowning Dill.

RANGER:

Umm, it is unlawful to swim naked in the lake.

LUCY:

And Lish walked out the lake, utterly naked and shimmering, looking like Joan of Arc.

LISH:

Unlawful?

RANGER:

Uh, yeah, as in, you're not supposed to do it.

LISH:

Not supposed to swim in this lake?

RANGER:

No, swimming's okay.

LISH:

So you're not supposed to be naked.

Lish poses fetchingly. The ranger melts.

RANGER:

Right now, I don't see a whole lot wrong with it.

LUCY:

They stood there, chatting and smiling at each other. Lish moved her hair around got some water on the ranger's pants, and then she made a big deal of wiping them off. The ranger looked up to the sky as if to say—

RANGER:

Thank you, Lord, for this naked woman rubbing my thigh.

LUCY:

And they shook hands. And the ranger left.

LISH:

That's that.

LUCY:

Cute ranger.

LISH:

I thought so.

LUCY:

I guess we didn't get a ticket.

LISH:

Of course not.

LUCY:

We could have, though.

LISH:

Never confuse Authority (*makes a salute*) with Power (*grabs her breasts*). They are not the same things at all.

LUCY AND LISH:

Authority (*make a salute*) with Power (*grab their breasts*).

The lights dim. Lucy and Lish sit in the van. A very friendly Canadian border guard runs on.

LUCY:

The next day we crossed the border into Canada. It was a breeze. They had to let us in, even if they didn't want to.

GUARD:

Did you purchase any firearms, telephones or pets?

LISH:

Yes, and a large quantity of lesbian porn, as well as drugs we were hoping to sell in schoolyards.

Hands her a mime cup of coffee.

GUARD:

Have a free Tim Horton's!

LISH:

Thanks!

LUCY:

And in we went. Pretty soon we passed the honey sign.

LISH:

Do you want to stop?

LUCY:

...No. And by the time I cheered up, we were approaching Winnipeg city limits.

LISH:

Look at that.

LUCY:

They had put up a sign that said—

An actor (as the Sign) appears behind the scrim, left.

SIGN:

Congratulations, Winnipeg! You survived!

LUCY:

Seems the flood was drying up. The disaster was over. There was a picture of a family of mosquitoes with suitcases, like they were about to leave town.

The actor holds a plunger to his face so he looks like a mosquito.

SIGN:

Bite rate down from forty-eight per minute to two!

LISH:

Well, that oughta bring in the tourists.

LUCY:

The shining sun made everything look different. Especially Have-a-Life. There were kids everywhere, playing and drawing in chalk on the concrete. There was something in the air. Something was going on.

They pull into Have-a-Life. SFX of kids playing. They wave at people and honk the horn. Naomi runs in, all aflutter.

LUCY:

As we pulled in, I saw Naomi running towards the van. She seemed in a big hurry to get her cheap American smokes. But that wasn't it.

NAOMI:

Guys, we need you.

LISH:

For what?

NAOMI:

Sarah's in *labour*!

LISH:

What?

NAOMI:

Sarah's in labour and she won't go to the hospital. She wants to have the baby in the apartment, but she won't get in the tub until it's sterilized and the midwife is late and we didn't even know she was pregnant. (*Naomi calms down for a second*) Did you know she was pregnant?

LISH AND LUCY:

No!

NAOMI:

Okay, so take the kids to Terrapin's and get scrubbing. We need every hand on scrubbing because Sing already boiled water.

LISH:

Why did Sing boil water?

NAOMI:

It's tradition!

Naomi exits at a run. She quick-changes into Dad.

LISH:

Holy shit.

LUCY:

What do we do?

LISH:

What we're told.

Dad enters and crouches at the toy box, scrubbing it.

LUCY:

And so I went into Sarah's bathroom and guess who's there? You'll never guess. I'll just tell you. My dad!

DAD:

(*quite flustered*) Hello, Lucy. It's quite busy here.

LUCY:

Hi, Dad. What are you doing here?

DAD:

The toilet at the house just exploded. It smelled quite terrible, and I knew your place was empty, so I convinced your Mr. Dylan to let me in. I've been staying there, and that Naomi lady found me and put me to work. I'm getting close to done here and then I am to rip some sheets up into strips.

LUCY:

Why?

DAD:

Apparently, it's tradition.

LUCY:

Isn't that how it goes, sometimes? People on the outside are so suddenly, so completely part of your life.

DAD:

I should tell you, I had need to contact a friend of yours. He's in the other room, trying to find the midwife.

LUCY:

I had never even heard him say the word pregnant before. He always said expecting. Now, here he was, ready to get placenta on his hands.

DAD:

A lawyer friend. A Mr. Weinstein? I found his business card in your bedroom. Sing was going to be sued for digging a trench—I'm just doing what I'm told.

Dad changes into Hart, grabbing the toy phone on his way to the table.

LUCY:

So I wandered to the phone in the kitchen and there was Hart.

HART:

(*on the phone*) Please hurry.

LUCY:

Hartley Weinstein, attorney at law.

HART:

Hey, Lucy.

LUCY:

Hart, what—

HART:

Your dad called me. Sing was going to be sued by the residents of Serenity Place. I guess he dug a trench—

LUCY:

The trench!

HART:

Some trench that carried all the flood water away from Have-a-Life, and right into Serenity Place. It led right to the unit belonging to a Sindy McCormican, but the whole place flooded. The entire complex.

LUCY:

Revenge was his. Honour was satisfied.

HART:

But I convinced them that they were better off getting flood benefits than suing a poor person. There's never a lot of profit in suing a poor person.

LUCY:

I guess not.

HART:

It's one of the main benefits. You know, of being poor.

LUCY:

Yeah. And then Hart to me looked like an outlaw crossed with a superhero. He looked like Robin Hood, but not as gay. He looked back and we just stood like that for a long time.

Hart picks up the Lego box with the crumpled tent in it.

HART:

I, uh— I have to start ripping these sheets into strips.

LUCY:

Why?

HART:

I don't know.

Hart smiles and exits at a run. Lucy smiles and then starts to cry.

LUCY:

And I started to cry. You might be getting tired of all the crying, but there's nothing I can do and this is the last of it. So much happens, so much happens all the time and things change so fast and it had been three years since Mom died, and how could I remember her with all this going on? How could I hold on to something so slender, when the ground is moving under my shoes?

Sarah enters, in her grey sweater, a blanket under it to denote her advanced pregnancy.

SARAH:

Ooooooooooow!

LUCY:

Just then, Sarah came around the corner.

SARAH:

What the fuck, Lucy! Is it ready?

LUCY:

She sure wasn't mute anymore.

SARAH:

(*contraction*) Ooooooooooow! Dammit, Lucy! Is the bathtub ready, or not? I'm gonna burst over here.

LUCY:

You won't burst, Sarah. It's okay.

SARAH:

This is happening, Lucy. This is happening right now

LUCY:

And even though I knew she meant her baby, I felt like maybe she also meant life. Life was happening. Right here and now.

SARAH:

This baby is going to be born any second!

LUCY:

And then she was swarmed by single mothers and hustled into the tub. The baby popped out not five minutes later.

Naomi enters and they sit Sarah down in the bathtub. They spin the bathtub and Sarah pulls out the blanket. She has given birth. Naomi turns into Sing Dylan, hiding her scarf amongst the baby's blanket. He is tearful. He and Sarah share a moment.

LUCY:

And she was beautiful. Milk chocolate brown and all Sing and Sarah. There was so much love flying between the three of them right then. Enough to light a country. Enough to light the world.

Sing helps Sarah up. He turns into Hart with a baby. Sarah takes off her sweater and becomes Lish.

After, we sat and drank coffee and played with the kids. Stunned into silence. Awestruck.

HART:

Who's a little monkey?

LUCY:

Hart was playing with Dill, pretending to chew his toes off.

HART:

You're a crazy little monkey!

Hart chews Dill's toes. He turns and puts on his glasses to become Dad.

LUCY:

Dad was laughing at a joke of Naomi's.

DAD:

Oh, that's filthy. (*he covers the baby's ears*)

LUCY:

My dad, midwife to the poor.

Lish makes a bird against the scrim. It flies off. Lish exits.

LUCY:

I saw Lish make a shadow puppet in a square of sunlight on Sarah's wall. If my mother had been in this apartment, she would have reflected happiness.

Mom appears behind the scrim, right.

MOM:

A good life, this. Happy and lucky. Good.

LUCY:

That night there was a tequila Scrabble party planned to celebrate all the good news. Sarah's baby, Sing not being sued, and Naomi saving the child tax credit.

Naomi appears behind the scrim, on the phone.

NAOMI:

Meet me in the alley, behind the Try 'N Save.

LUCY:

Oh, yeah, Naomi totally blackmailed Bunnie. Like it was a movie or something.

Bunnie appears behind the scrim, right.

BUNNIE:

What do you want?

NAOMI:

I want you to keep the child tax credit in place for mothers on welfare. Or your little insurance scam goes to every BLEEP-ing paper in the country.

BUNNIE:

Well, aren't you crafty?

NAOMI:

From you, that's a BLEEP-ing compliment.

BUNNIE:

You've got a foul mouth.

NAOMI:

Yeah? Well, you're a BLEEP.

BUNNIE:

(*flinching*) You got a deal.

Naomi nods, smiling, giving Bunnie the finger. Lights out on them.

LUCY:

Naomi might have embellished the story a little. She does that sometimes. But how awesome is that, right? Fifteen hundred extra dollars for all of us. And that's what Bunnie gets for lying. Which brings me to Lish.

Lish reels onto stage, quite hammered.

LISH:

I'm not a mean drunk.

LUCY:

It was at the tequila party. A little later in the night.

LISH:

I am sometimes mean and I am sometimes drunk, but I am not a mean drunk.

LUCY:

The warm feelings still hung in the air. And then—

LISH:

Oh, my God, Lucy— Look!

LUCY:

What?

LISH:

Over there! It's a miracle!

LUCY:

What?

LISH:

It's him! It's Gotcha! He's alive!

LUCY:

Lish—

LISH:

Oh! Here he is in my pocket!

LUCY:

Lish, I—

LISH:

No, no! He's behind your EAR!

Lish pulls him out from behind Lucy's ear like a magic trick.

LISH:

(*smiling*) Gotcha!

Lish laughs and laughs and then suddenly passes out.

LUCY:

And then she passed out. My heart fell into my stomach. The jig was up. Now the truth would be out and Lish would hate me and I'd have to move out, probably to Serenity Place and I'd be a bitter aging welfare mom with no friends at all. I was ready for the worst when Lish finally woke up the next day.

LISH:

Gotcha.

LUCY:

How did you know?

LISH:

The silver spoon was my first clue. I took it after he was gone. He wouldn't've known about it.

LUCY:

Right.

LISH:

Then I got to thinking. Gunned down outside a movie theatre? Exactly like somebody's favorite outlaw?

LUCY:

John Dillinger.

LISH:

John Dillinger.

LUCY:

You're quite a detective.

LISH:

I'm J. Edgar Hoover. But not as gay.

LUCY:

I am so sorry, Lish. You were just so sad and I got so scared and it all got so out of hand, and I wanted to be supportive of your trip, even if I knew, and then there we were, and I thought maybe it was better that he be dead, instead of—

LISH:

Instead of just out there.

LUCY:

Yeah.

LISH:

Maybe it is better.

LUCY:

Yeah?

LISH:

I've decided. It's better.

LUCY:

I'm so sorry, Lish.

LISH:

I know, and lying sucks.

LUCY:

I know.

LISH:

It does. But I forgive you. That's how it's supposed to go, with family.

LUCY:

But we're not—

LISH:

Shut up, Lucy. This is mushy enough.

They laugh together and Lish gets up painfully, suffering from her hangover.

LUCY:

So my prayer came true. We laughed about it someday. Today.

Dad stayed at my house for a few days more. During the day he would watch the workmen at his house, and at supper he would take us to restaurants. Always for burgers. I think because I was frozen at fourteen in his head. I didn't mind. Burgers were my favourite, back before Mom died and I didn't grieve right. We ate and sometimes we talked and sometimes we didn't. But there we were. There we were.

Dad comes around the corner. He accepts the presents from the women and moves down to Lucy.

When Dad was ready to go back home, Terrapin gave him some laxative tea, and Naomi gave him some American smokes, in case he wanted to start. They drifted away and Dad took my hand. It was dry and soft and very big. Just like Dill's hands. I could see where he fit in.

DAD:

Well—

LUCY:

Dad, how come you and Mom didn't have any more kids?

DAD:

Well, it just didn't happen.

LUCY:

And he smiled, as if to say he understood now that sometime kids do happen. They just happen.

DAD:

Lucy—

LUCY:

Yeah?

DAD:

Life is not a joke.

LUCY:

No.

DAD:

No.

LUCY:

No. But it's funny.

DAD:

Yes. And Dill.

LUCY:

Yeah?

DAD:

He's a lucky boy.

LUCY:

You think?

DAD:

He's a lucky boy.

Dad kisses her cheek and exits.

DAD:

See you later.

LUCY:

See you soon.

DAD:

See you soon.

LUCY:

And he left, and I stayed. At home. At Have-a-Life. Winnipeg, Manitoba, Canada. Most hours of sunshine. Centre of the world. Life is not a joke. But it's funny. And Dillinger Jeffery Van Alstyne is lucky. He's a lucky boy, after all.

The End

Chris Craddock graduated from the University of Alberta's BFA Acting Program in 1996. He has acted for many theatres all over Canada, and is the author of several plays for audiences of many categories. These include *SuperEd, Indulgences, The "Tranny" Trilogy* (with Darrin Hagen), *The Day Billy Lived, Wrecked, Do it Right, Making Out, Men are Stupid, Women are Crazy, Ha!* (with Wes Borg), *PornStar, BoyGroove* (songs and lyrics by Aaron Macri), *3... 2...1* (with Nathan Cuckow), *DreamLife, Moving Along* (recently featured on Bravo) and this adaptation of the novel *Summer of my Amazing Luck* by Miriam Toews. Chris is the former Artistic Director of Azimuth Theatre and the current Artistic Director of Rapid Fire Theatre. He has been nominated for a total of 14 of Edmonton's Sterling awards and won four. His first film, *Turnbuckle,* was nominated for two AMPIA Awards. Chris is also the winner of the Alberta Book Award, the Embridge Award for Best Emerging Artist, and a 2005 Alberta Centennial Medal for his contribution to the arts in Alberta.

Québec, Canada
2007